Who Am I?

Who Am I?

Clue-by-Clue Biographical
Sketches of American
Historical Figures

by MARSHA LYNN BEEMAN

McFarland & Company, Inc., Publishers
Jefferson, North Carolina, and London

Photos of Lillian Gish, Rita Hayworth, Gloria Swanson and
George M. Cohan courtesy of Film Favorites; photos of William
H. Taft, Henry Ford, Althea Gibson and Luther Burbank
courtesy of Raymond Fardy. All other photographs courtesy of
National Portrait Gallery, Washington, D.C./Art Resource, N.Y.

British Library Cataloguing-in-Publication data are available

Library of Congress Cataloguing-in-Publication Data

Beeman, Marsha Lynn, 1959–
    Who am I? : clue-by-clue biographical sketches of American
historical figures / by Marsha Lynn Beeman.
        p. cm.
    Includes bibliographical references and index.
    ISBN 0-89950-899-5 (sewn softcover : 50# alk. paper) ∞
    1. United States—Biography. 2. Leadership. 3. Questions and
answers. 4. Curiosities and wonders. I. Title.
CT214.B44 1993
920'.073—dc20   92-56629
                                                             CIP

Manufactured in the United States of America

McFarland & Company, Inc., Publishers
  Box 611, Jefferson, North Carolina 28640

God has blessed me with a wonderful family. Growing up, there were five very special individuals who are responsibile for who I am today. It is in loving memory that I dedicate this book to them: my grandmother, Daisy Hazel (Shimer) Beeman; my father, William Wesley Beeman, Sr.; and two aunts, Hattie May Beeman and Mary Elizabeth (Beeman) Preston.

To my mother, Catherine, I am so thankful I still have you with me.

Contents

Introduction

Who Am I? describes 144 people who were born in the United States. A total of 720 stimulating clues will test the reader's proficiency at gaining knowledge about them.

Each famous person is given a brief biography and five clues. The collection of clues allows the reader to arrive at the true identity of the famous person through a natural progression. Some clues may need more thought, unless the reader is already familiar with the person. A summary of correct answers is at the back of the book, along with three sources for further reading for each person.

Looking for an educational game for your classroom or get together? Tired of reruns, and looking for something for the whole family to do? How about a game of trivia with a new twist? *Who Am I?* can be used as a game to be played by one or two individuals or groups. Players must guess the identity of a noteworthy American from the five clues per person. There are 12 persons in each of the 12 chapters.

Have your game players pair up—or for larger gatherings have one group match wits against another. Players alternate turns; the first team gets the first five clues (one clue at a time) from Chapter One, then the next team receives their five clues from the same chapter. Players are given clues in Chapter One, then Two, and so forth through the 12 chapters. After the twelfth chapter, players can return to Chapter One to repeat the process until a couple or team reaches, say, 200 points. Scoring can be as follows: 25 points for giving the correct answer upon being offered the first clue; 20 points for answering correctly on the second clue; 15 points for answering correctly on the third clue; 10 points for answering correctly on the fourth clue; and 5 points for answering correctly after getting the fifth and last clue. If a player or team offers an incorrect answer (no matter what clue they are on) no penalty need be incurred. The next player or team has the opportunity to pick up those points for providing a correct answer – and gets a regular turn as well!

Another version of this game again has players divided into teams. One player stands up in front of their team (like the game of charades) to become a mystery person. Players can use mannerisms, voices, or whatever they can come up with to help their teammates reveal the identity of the mystery person at the earliest clue. Scoring is the same as before. If the team fails to identify the mystery person correctly on the fifth and final clue, then the other team has the opportunity to steal 25 points. The first team to reach 200 points is the winner. Remember to use every resource you can think of to get your team to guess the identity of the mystery person.

Who Am I? can also be played in a two stage form. In stage one, players are given one of the 12 chapters (for instance, Presidents) as their topic. Two dice are then thrown to determine the number of presidents a player must list on a piece of paper. For each correct answer a player receives five points. In stage two, a player is given five clues for as many famous persons (for instance, African Americans) as the number that was previously thrown on the dice. After hearing the final clue, the player must then write down the famous person's name. Players receive ten points for each correct answer. This procedure is followed for all 12 sections. At the end of the twelfth section, the player with the highest score wins.

Another game idea using this book: Have players sit in a circle. Spin a bottle to see who begins the game. Then five clues from a famous person are read from any of the book's 12 sections. After the last clue is read, a player has 30 seconds to respond. If a player correctly identifies the famous person, that player stays in the circle and spins the bottle. A new famous person is chosen and the five clues are read. If a player offers an incorrect identification, he or she must leave the circle. The player to the right must then guess the identity of this person. If this player answers correctly, the game proceeds by having the player spin the bottle. If this player incorrectly answers, players to the right shall take turns in order of their seating around the circle, until there is a correct answer. Each time an incorrect answer is given, the player who gave the wrong answer must leave the circle. Play continues until there is one player left: the winner of the game.

In a different version, have players sit in a circle. To start the game, pass out a playing card (from any card deck) to each player. The player with the lowest card goes first. This player is given five clues to the identity of a famous person from any of the 12 chapters. After the last clue is read, the player has 30 seconds to respond. If the player correctly identifies the famous person, he or she stays in the circle. The next player to the right takes a turn next. If the player incorrectly identifies the famous person, that player must leave the circle. The next player to the right would be given 30 seconds to respond. This process is continued around the circle, until one player is left in the circle.

All of these versions of *Who Am I?* can be played at home or in the classroom. For fun, have students make up their own rules. Here are some other classroom ideas for busy teachers and librarians.

During Black History Month, display a bulletin board with clues about African Americans (Chapter Three). To pique students' interest, include silhouettes of the African Americans chosen. Under each silhouette, list the five clues associated with that person. In the last week of the month, reveal the identities of these famous African Americans by placing their photograph over their silhouette. On the last day of the month, reveal their name under their last clue. Besides learning more about African Americans, this exercise will allow students to associate a name with a face.

To stimulate the minds of history students, select a famous American each week from any of the book's chapters. Then each day write a new clue on the blackboard, until all five clues have been used. On Friday, have students guess who the mystery person is.

For a science class activity, prepare a worksheet using clues from the chapter on Inventors (Chapter Seven). Have students look up information from various sources to answer clues. This activity can be done as a library project or in the classroom. If it is completed in the classroom, be sure to provide reference books for research.

In a music class, have students listen to various pieces of music associated with one of the Musicians/Composers (Chapter Eight). After the music has been played, begin reading the five clues associated with that famous person. Once each clue is read, allow students time to guess their identity. This is a wonderful opportunity for students to appreciate the music of famous Americans, while learning more about them as individuals.

For an art class activity, have students look at five slides of art work associated with one of the Artists (Chapter Eleven). As each work is projected onto the screen, read one clue associated with that artist. That is, one clue for each slide until all five clues have been read. Then have students write down the identity of each artist on a piece of paper that has been numbered 1 through 12. Turn on the lights and compare answers. This procedure can also be used as a test.

In an English class, have students choose from any of the chapters a famous person on whom they would like to write a biography. Students will need time in the library to do research. Once the research has been completed and the papers written, have students present them to the class. While the students present their papers, have the rest of the class take notes. After all the papers have been presented, give students a quiz based on the five clues associated with each famous person that has been presented to the class.

Who Am I? could also be used to add a little fun to a remedial reading class or as part of the Literacy Plus Program. Have one of your students read each of the five clues out loud. After the last clue has been read, have students guess the famous person's identity.

Sports is an all-time favorite, so I have devoted two chapters to these participants. The chapters are roughly divided (with some overlap). Try selections from both! Display photographs and clues of Sports Figures (Chapter Five) and Heroes of the Olympic Games (Chapter Twelve) on a bulletin board. Place photographs on the left, clues on the right. Label photographs numerically and clues alphabetically. Mix photographs and clues, so that students have to match the clues with the famous person's picture. Set a time span (for instance, one week, two weeks) for students to correctly match photograph numbers with clue letters. When time expires, rearrange the bulletin board so that photographs are matched with clues. For example, under each photograph place the five clues that correspond to that famous person.

I hope you find these suggestions useful and the games or activities entertaining. It was my intention in writing this book that it would be a challenging way to spend an evening, or a fun learning experience for students. If I have accomplished this goal, then I have been successful.

Marsha Beeman
Fall 1992

Chapter One

Presidents

1 In 1776, as a member of the Continental Congress, I was chosen to draft the Declaration of Independence. Through my skills as a committeeman and draftsman, I gained national recognition. Twenty years later, the Republicans supported me for President, although I was considered a founder of the Democratic party. After losing by a mere three electoral votes to John Adams, I became his Vice President. In the next Presidential election (1800), the tables were turned and I defeated John Adams to become the third President of the United States. My greatest accomplishment during my presidency (1801–1809) was the Louisiana Purchase in 1803 at a cost of $15 million.

I was born on April 13, 1743, in Shadwell, Virginia, to a prominent Virginia family. As a child, I attended small private schools. Later I attended the College of William and Mary, where I graduated in 1762. After graduation I read law with George Wythe in Virginia for the next five years and was admitted to the bar in 1767. I practiced law until 1774. It was during these years that my interests turned toward writing and politics. My life ended on July 4, 1826, at my home (Monticello) on the 50th anniversary of the Declaration of Independence.

WHO AM I?

1. I was born on April 13, 1743, in Shadwell, Virginia, to a prominent Virginia family.
2. George Wythe accepted me as his law student. I later laid out the plans for the University of Virginia.
3. I commissioned Meriwether Lewis and William Clark to explore the

Louisiana Territory, which was bought from Napoleon Bonaparte of
France for $15 million while I was President.
4. I served as a Republican Vice President under John Adams, a Federal-
   ist, marking the only time President and Vice President were from different political parties.
5. I drafted the Declaration of Independence in 1776. In my later years,
   I retired to my home, Monticello.

2 While serving as Minister to Great Britain (appointed to the post by President Pierce in 1853), I
was nominated by the Democrats as their Presidential
candidate. In 1856, I defeated the Republican candidate John C. Fremont to become the 15th President
of the United States. My administration (1857–1861) was highly criticized
for the Dred Scott Decision and the handling of John Brown's attack on
Harper's Ferry on October 16, 1859. Our nation did move forward during
my four years: the Pony Express was established, the Atlantic cable was
laid, there was a gold strike in Colorado, and three new states (Minnesota,
Oregon, and Kansas) were added to the Union.

My life began on April 23, 1791, on a farm near Mercersburg, Pennsylvania. School was a very important part of my life, which I proved as
a student at Dickinson College. In 1812 I became a lawyer, but I gave it
up to enlist in the army (as a private) when the British threatened to attack
Baltimore. After the war I served in Congress (1820), then as Minister to
Russia (1830), as a Senator (1833), and as Secretary of State (1845) in
Polk's Cabinet. Then I retired for five years but came out of retirement to
accept President Pierce's appointment. Discouraged with politics after my
presidency, I returned to my home in Lancaster, Pennsylvania, where I
("Old Buck") died on June 1, 1868, at the age of 77.

WHO AM I?

1. I was born on April 23, 1791, on a farm near Mercersburg, Pennsylvania.
2. During my administration, the Pony Express was established, the
   Atlantic cable was laid, there was a gold strike in Colorado, and three
   new states (Minnesota, Oregon and Kansas) were added to the Union.

3. I defeated the new Republican Party's candidate, John C. Fremont, to become the 15th President of the United States.
4. I was the only President to remain a bachelor (never married).
5. I was nicknamed "Old Buck."

3

My political career began at the age of 28, when I scored an impressive win as a candidate for the New York State Senate in 1910. Ten years later, as a Vice Presidential nominee, I was beaten resoundingly. After serving two terms as Governor of New York, I decided to run for President in the 1932 campaign. I was able to beat President Hoover (22,821,857 to 15,761,841 votes and 472 to 59 electoral votes) to become the 32nd President of the United States; I was reelected for an unprecedented three more terms. The Great Depression hampered my administration, but I was able to push through my New Deal, which created the Works Progress Administration (WPA) that provided $11 million in work relief for over three million Americans.

I began my life of privilege on January 30, 1882, at our family compound in Hyde Park, New York. My early education was provided by governesses and private tutors. At the age of 14 I attended Groton School in Massachusetts. I moved on to Harvard and graduated in three years with my B.A. in 1903. Then I studied law at Columbia, but quit. I passed the New York bar exam and worked with a Wall Street law firm, but found it too routine so I moved on to politics like my uncle-in-law before me. I lived and breathed politics (often hampered by polio) until it became too much for my heart on April 12, 1945, in Warm Springs, Georgia, at the age of 63.

WHO AM I?

1. I was born on January 30, 1882, in Hyde Park, New York.
2. I was the first President to appear on national television.
3. During my presidency, Japan bombed Pearl Harbor on December 7, 1941.
4. I held the office of President longer than any other President: twelve years, one month and eight days.
5. My fifth-cousin Teddy gave our nation "the Square Deal." I gave our nation "the New Deal."

4

The service of my country was always foremost in my life. On August 2, 1943, a Japanese destroyer ripped my PT boat in half. As a superb swimmer, I was able to save the lives of my ten crew members. For my efforts, I received the Purple Heart and the Navy and Marine Corps Medal. In 1952 (relying on my war record), I looked toward politics and defeated Henry Cabot Lodge to gain a seat in the United States Senate. Four years later, I almost won the Democratic Vice Presidential nomination. The year 1960 proved more successful, and I became the first Roman Catholic and youngest (43 years old) man to occupy the office of President by defeating Richard M. Nixon in a close popular vote race. My short administration saw the establishment of the

Peace Corps and the Cuban Missile Crisis, which prompted Soviet Premier Khrushchev to dismantle the missiles he had had installed in Cuba after I ordered a naval blockade of the island.

I was born into politics on May 29, 1917, in Brookline, Massachusetts. My early school years at the Canterbury School and Choate School were less scholarly than my older brother Joe's. Despite my father's wishes (he was a Harvard man), I entered Princeton. After a summer in London and an illness, I ended up at Harvard, where I graduated with honors in political science. The writer in me produced two books: *While England Slept*, a best-seller, and *Profiles in Courage*, which won a Pulitzer Prize in history for 1957. Politics consumed my life until an assassin's bullet ended it in Dallas, Texas, on November 22, 1963.

WHO AM I?

1. I was born on May 29, 1917, in Brookline, Massachusetts.
2. My grandfather, "Honey Fitz," was mayor of Boston, one of many elective offices he held.
3. I won the 1957 Pulitzer Prize in history for my book, *Profiles in Courage*.
4. I was the first Roman Catholic elected to the Presidency.
5. I was the youngest President to die in office, at the age of 46, from an assassin's bullet on November 22, 1963, in Dallas, Texas.

5 On Palm Sunday, April 1865, I met Robert E. Lee at the Appomattox Court House to shake hands on an agreement of surrender by the Confederates. My success in the Civil War provided me with eight troubled years in the White House. Carpetbaggers were rampant in the South, graft and greed ruled our government, Black Friday and the Panic of 1873 almost destroyed our nation financially, and I was accused of being a part of the gold scheme that brought about these two events. My administration did have its positive moments, such as when the 15th Amendment was adopted, Yellowstone National Park was established, the first transcontinental railroad was finished, and Colorado was admitted to the Union.

My life began as "Hiram" on April 27, 1822, in Point Pleasant, Ohio.

Education was not a priority, my love of horses was. I attended various subscription schools until the age of 17, at which time I received an appointment to West Point. My father was delighted; I would have rather taught mathematics than be a soldier. It was not until the Mexican War that I found out that I was a good soldier and that I liked it. After the war I turned to farming and my father's leather business, which I did out of necessity. Then the Civil War called and once again I became a soldier (general). My life was ended by throat cancer on July 23, 1885, one week after I finished my memoirs.

WHO AM I?

1. I was ruined financially when I went into partnership with Ferdinand Ward in the banking business.
2. I died of throat cancer on July 23, 1885, in Mount McGregor, New York.
3. On April 27, 1822, in Point Pleasant, Ohio, I was given the first name "Hiram."
4. During my eight years in office, the 15th Amendment was adopted, Colorado was admitted to the Union, and Yellowstone National Park became our first national park, but my administration was marred by the Panic of 1873, Black Friday, and fraud in the government.
5. At West Point, I was entered on the attendance rolls as "U.S.," nicknamed "Uncle Sam," then just plain "Sam."

6 In the 1912 Presidential campaign, I won the Democratic nomination on the 48th ballot. The Republicans had a split ticket that year with Roosevelt and Taft. I scored a resounding victory with 6,286,214 votes over Roosevelt's 4,216,020 and Taft's 3,482,922. My first administration saw many changes: a graduated income tax was installed (incomes under $3,000 were exempt), a tariff bill lowered duties, the Federal Reserve Act was introduced, the Federal Trade Commission ended various unfair trade practices, and the Pure Food Law protected consumers. Four years later, I won reelection against Chief Justice Charles Evans Hughes (a very powerful Republican candidate) in a close electoral vote of 277 to 254. My second administration saw

Congress declare war on Germany on Good Friday, April 1917, my famous speech titled "Fourteen Points" outlining fourteen steps for a peace settlement, and my greatest dream of all came true when the League of Nations was established. With my two administrations, I was able to keep Congress in session longer than any other President.

My life began on December 28, 1856, in Staunton, Virginia. The Civil War kept me from attending school until I was nine years old. My poor eyesight and health forced me to drop out of Davidson College during my freshman year. But I did not let this setback get me down, and I graduated from Princeton University and attended the University of Virginia to study law. As a lawyer in Atlanta, Georgia, I had few clients, so I went to Johns Hopkins University to attend graduate school to become a college professor. I taught at Bryn Mawr College, Wesleyan University, and Princeton, where I became its president. But in 1910, politics called and I became Governor of New Jersey. On February 3, 1924, I died at my home in Washington, DC.

WHO AM I?

1. My life began on December 28, 1856 in Staunton, Virginia; the Civil War kept me from attending school until I was nine.
2. With my two administrations, I was able to keep Congress in session longer than any other President.
3. I am the only President to have earned a doctoral degree (Ph.D.), which I received from Johns Hopkins University.
4. I was the first President to talk on the radio.
5. I took my "Fourteen Points" to the Paris Peace Conference, which provided a peace settlement to end World War I.

7

In 1880, I won the Republican nomination over Grant and two other men. Then I went on to beat my Democratic opponent, General Winfield Scott Hancock, in the general election. One year later, Booker T. Washington opened the Tuskegee Institute and Clara Barton organized the American Red Cross. Early in July of that same year, my administration was cut short by an assassin's bullet as I walked through the waiting room of the Baltimore & Potomac station. I was

scheduled to deliver the commencement address at Williams College that day, but Charles J. Guiteau had other plans as he fired two shots at my back. For the next ten weeks I lingered, then I lapsed into unconsciousness and succumbed to blood-poisoning on September 19, 1881, in Elberon, New Jersey.

My life began much more quietly on November 19, 1831, in Orange (Cuyahoga County), Ohio. I learned to read at the age of three. By the time I was 14, I was a good student with a knack for grammar and arithmetic. I also was a strong young man who found work as a carpenter, farm hand, and mule driver. I left these jobs to return to my passion—education. I spent a semester at Geagua Seminary, then attended Hiram Eclectic Institute, where I taught English and ancient studies to pay my way, and in 1856 I graduated from Williams with top honors. In the following six years, I became a college president (Hiram), state senator, a major-general in the Civil War (Union army), and a member-elect for Congress.

WHO AM I?

1. I was born on November 19, 1831, in Orange (Cuyahoga County), Ohio, the last President to be born in a log cabin.
2. As a young man I drove mules along the Ohio canal and spent time as a carpenter. Later, I served as a college president at Hiram Eclectic Institute, served as a state senator, and was a major general in the Civil War (Union army).
3. As a congressman, I was known as the "champion of the 'hard-money' men."
4. While I was in office, Tuskegee Institute was opened by Booker T. Washington and Clara Barton organized the American Red Cross.
5. I was shot by Charles J. Guiteau in the waiting room of the Baltimore & Potomac railroad station. Ten weeks later, I succumbed to blood-poisoning on September 19, 1881, in Elberon, New Jersey.

8 In 1945 (during World War II), I commanded "Operation Overlord," considered to be the greatest military invasion in our history. Riding my popularity as a war hero, I became the 34th President of the United States (the first Texan and the third army man to do so), defeating Republican Adlai Stevenson by more than six-and-half million votes. In 1956, I won a second term by again easily defeating Adlai Stevenson. I turned 70 that year, making me the first President to attain that age. My greatest achievement of my presidency came in July 1953, when I ended the Korean War, which cost our nation 33,237 lives. Heart attacks plagued my last year of life (even in 1955 when I was President); I took my final breath on March 28, 1969, in Washington, DC.

My life began on October 14, 1890, in Denison, Texas, but we soon moved to Abilene, Kansas where I eventually attended high school. There I played football and baseball, preferring football above all. At the age of 25, I was unable to get an appointment to the Naval Academy, because I was past the age limit of 20. Gaining an appointment to West Point, I once again played football. But a football injury ended my career on the field and almost ended my military career (the medical board considered my fitness for a military commission).

I received a commission and became a lieutenant-colonel during World War I, but I was reduced to major in 1920 (a rank I held for the next sixteen years). I never gave up, I did my duty and ended my military career as a five-star general.

WHO AM I?

1. My life began on October 14, 1890, in Denison, Texas.
2. I played football at West Point, until a knee injury sidelined me.
3. In 1945 (during World War II), I commanded "Operation Overlord."
4. In 1956, I won a second term by easily defeating Adlai Stevenson. I turned 70 that year, making me the first President to attain that age.
5. I was given the nickname "Ike."

In 1908, Teddy Roosevelt pushed me into the Presidential nomination, which I easily won over William Jennings Bryan to become the 27th President of the United States. The next four years were busy years for my administration: Arizona and New Mexico were admitted to the Union, Henry Ford mass-produced his Model T, Robert E. Peary and Ronald Amundsen reached the North and South Poles respectively, Alaska was granted a territorial government, Parcel Post and Postal Savings were established, along with the Department of Labor and the Federal Children's Fund, and two new amendments were added to the Constitution (16th a Federal Income Tax and 17th establishing a popular election for United States Senators). In 1912, after losing the Republican nomination, I left Washington to return to my first love — law (as a professor of law at Yale).

I was born on September 15, 1857, in Cincinnati, Ohio. I rose through the public schools to attend Yale (my father's alma mater) and graduated second in my class. My love for the law began as an assistant prosecutor and assistant solicitor for Hamilton County. I moved through the ranks of judgeship, first as a judge in the Ohio Supreme Court, U.S. Solicitor General, then as a judge on the Federal Court of Appeals (appointed by President Harrison). I was named Chief Justice of the Supreme Court in 1921 (made me the only person in history to hold the two highest offices of President and Chief Justice). After eight years on the court, I was forced to retire due to poor health. A month later, I ("Big Bill") died on March 8, 1930, in Washington, DC.

WHO AM I?

1. I was born on September 15, 1857, in Cincinnati, Ohio.
2. During my term in office, the 16th Amendment established a Federal Income Tax.

3. I served as both President and Chief Justice of the Supreme Court. As Chief Justice, I gave the Oath of Office to two of my successors, Calvin Coolidge and Herbert Hoover.
4. My friends called me "Big Bill."
5. I was the heaviest President, at 350 pounds (over six feet tall).

10

I was pushed into politics by the "Big Tom" Pendergast political machine. He went to the penitentiary, while I went on to be a judge and a United States Senator. The presidential campaign of 1944 changed my political destiny; 83 days after Roosevelt was elected to his fourth term, I assumed the office of President just weeks shy of my 61st birthday. My administration (1944–1952) was filled with difficult times: it saw the surrender of Germany, the signing of the Potsdam Declaration that called for the surrender of Japan, the decision to drop the first atomic bomb on Hiroshima and a second on Nagasaki to end the war, the signing of the North Atlantic Treaty Organization (NATO), the invasion of South Korea by North Korea on June 25, 1950, and the veto of the Taft-Hartley Labor Act by Congress, which later passed the same act.

My life began on May 8, 1884, in Lamar, Missouri. Those early years were hampered by my poor eyesight, which also kept me out of West Point. I tried my hand at odd jobs (a paper wrapper for the *Kansas City Star*, timekeeper on the Santa Fe Railroad, bank clerk, and bookkeeper), then returned home to run the family farm after my father's death. World War I called and I answered, becoming a major in the field artillery. After the war I entered into an unsuccessful haberdashery business, which was the final push into politics.

WHO AM I?

1. I was born on May 8, 1884, in Lamar, Missouri.
2. My one big failure in life was that my haberdashery business in Kansas City went bankrupt.
3. I defeated Thomas E. Dewey of New York to win reelection to my second term.
4. I was known as the "Man from Independence."
5. On August 6, 1945, I gave the command to drop the atomic bomb on

Hiroshima. Three days later, a second bomb was dropped on Nagasaki.

My "House Divided Speech" and my debates with Stephen Douglas brought me national recognition. When I came to the Presidency in 1861 (defeated William H. Seward on the third ballot), our nation was divided by the Civil War. Four bloody years of war were ended with the Emancipation Proclamation and the 13th Amendment, which abolished slavery. In 1864, I easily won a second term. But my second term was cut short, when John Wilkes Booth shot me in the back of the head in the Presidential box at Ford's Theater. The next morning, April 15, 1865, I died.

I was born on February 12, 1809, in Hardin County, Kentucky. When I was eight years old we moved to southwestern Indiana. Two years later, my mother died and my older sister Sarah took care of us. My stepmother Sarah insisted that I get an education, so I learned from traveling school teachers and borrowed books. After 14 years in Indiana (at the age of 21), I moved to Illinois. In 1831, I moved to New Salem where I helped in a store that eventually failed, studied surveying, worked as a postmaster, ran for the State Legislature and lost, and studied law from borrowed books. I moved to Springfield, where I was a lawyer and served in Congress for two years. Disgruntled with politics, I returned to Springfield and dropped out of the public eye. If it were not for the Kansas-Nebraska Bill and the Dred Scott decision, I would have never returned to politics.

WHO AM I?

1. My life began on February 12, 1809, in Hardin County, Kentucky.
2. I was defeated six times in my attempts for public office before becoming the 16th President of the United States.
3. My famous debates with Stephen A. Douglas brought me national recognition.
4. I was assassinated by John Wilkes Booth at Ford's Theater in Washington, DC.
5. I was given the nicknames of the "Illinois Rail Splitter," the "Great Emancipator," and "Honest Abe."

<table>
<tr><td>

12

</td><td>

As Governor of Ohio, I made sweeping changes that brought me national recognition, which was responsible for my win over William Jennings Bryan in the presidential election of 1896. Four years later, I was able to capture a second term over this same

</td></tr>
</table>

man. My administration will be best remembered for the battle cry "Remember the Maine" (a warship blown up in the Havana Harbor), the declaration of war on April 21, 1898, to begin the Spanish-American War (lasted 113 days), and the annexation of Hawaii. My second term was cut short by an assassin's bullet, while attending a reception at the Pan-American Exposition in Buffalo, New York. A young man named Leon Czolgosz fired two shots from his .32-caliber revolver, and I died eight days later, on September 14, 1901.

Life began quietly on January 29, 1843, in Niles, Ohio. After dropping out of Allegheny College in my junior year because of poor health, I taught school and worked as a postal clerk in Poland, Ohio. With the outbreak of the Civil War, I enlisted in the Ohio 23rd Volunteers. By the end of the war, President Lincoln had given me the rank of major. After the war I found my niche in law and politics. I progressed from a prosecuting attorney, to Congress (served twelve years), then to Governor of Ohio.

WHO AM I?

1. I was born on January 29, 1843, in Niles, Ohio.
2. I worked as a postal clerk in Poland, Ohio, when the Civil War broke out.
3. I was the last veteran of the Civil War to occupy the White House.
4. "Remember the Maine" was the battle cry when Congress declared war on April 21, 1898, to begin the Spanish-American War.
5. I was shot by Leon Czolgosz, while attending the Pan-American Exposition in Buffalo, New York. I died eight days later on September 14, 1901.

Chapter Two

Women

1

I worked diligently in the women's rights movement, almost up to my last breath trying to give women the right to vote. When I was 33, I gave my first speech for women's rights. This speech was given at the annual New York State Teachers Association convention (Rochester, New York) in 1853. In 1901, I campaigned to get the University of Rochester (New York) to accept women. Five years later, after returning home from my 86th birthday celebration and women's rights meeting in Washington, DC, I was stricken with pneumonia. On March 13, 1906, I died in Rochester, New York. Fourteen years after my death (1920), women were given the right to vote by the 19th Amendment to the Constitution, which was named in my honor.

My life began on February 15, 1820, in the Berkshire Hills near Adams, Massachusetts. In my early teens, my formal education began with a private tutor, then I went on to a Quaker finishing school near Philadelphia. After graduation I taught at an all girls boarding school in New Rochelle, New York. Later, I was the headmistress of the girls' department at the Canajoharie Academy, where I joined the Canajoharie Daughters of Temperance and became their president. For my exploits, newspaper reporters began calling me the "Woman Napoleon." The summer of 1856 saw my attentions turn to organizing antislavery meetings in Kansas to help John Brown. But my attentions soon turned back to my first love – women's rights.

WHO AM I?

1. I was born on February 15, 1820, in the Berkshire Hills near Adams, Massachusetts.

2. I taught at an all girls boarding school in New Rochelle, New York.
3. As headmistress of the girls' department at Canajoharie Academy, I joined the Canajoharie Daughters of Temperance.
4. For my exploits, newspaper reporters began calling me the "Woman Napoleon."
5. I gave my first speech on women's rights at the annual New York State Teachers Association convention in 1853. Fourteen years after my death on March 13, 1906, women were given the right to vote in the 19th Amendment to the Constitution, which was named in my honor.

2 On June 18, 1928, I became the first woman to cross the Atlantic by air. I was a passenger aboard the "Friendship" that day, with pilot Wilmer L. "Bill" Stultz and mechanic Louis "Slim" Gordon. The official flight time was 20 hours 40 minutes, but you will also see it recorded as 20 hours 49 minutes. That same year (September-October), I decided to go solo to make the first solo-return transcontinental flight by a woman. Nine years later, my aviation career came to a close after attempting a round-the-world flight from Oakland, California to Honolulu, Hawaii. It was on July 2, 1937, after completing 22,000 miles of the flight that my plane went down between Lae, New Guinea and Howland Island. I was never to be heard from again.

It all started on July 24, 1898, in Atchison, Kansas. As a child I was nicknamed "Millie" and my sister Muriel was known as "Pidge." In 1908 at the Iowa State Fair, I saw my first airplane and fell in love. While attending Columbia University in 1920, I took my first flight with Frank Hawks. One year later, I began taking flying lessons from Anita "Neta" Snook.

WHO AM I?

1. I was born on July 24, 1898, in Atchison, Kansas.
2. In 1918, I worked as a nurse in Toronto, Canada, at the Spadina Military Convalescent Hospital.
3. I took my first flight with Frank Hawks in 1920. One year later, I began taking flying lessons from Anita "Neta" Snook.
4. After completing 22,000 miles of my round-the-world flight with navigator Fred Noonan, I lost radio contact and was never seen again.
5. On June 18, 1928, I became the first woman to cross the Atlantic by air (with pilot Wilmer L. "Bill" Stultz and mechanic Louis "Slim" Gordon in the airplane "Friendship"), after 20 hours and 40 minutes. I was nicknamed "Lady Lindy."

3   When the Civil War broke out in 1861, I delivered supplies and offered aid to wounded soldiers out of my pocket. This altruism earned me the names "Angel of the Battlefield" and the "Yankee Florence Nightingale." After the war I supervised a search program for missing soldiers and lived in Europe (1869–1873) establishing hospitals for Germany during the Franco-German War. For my efforts, I was honored with the Gold Cross of Baden and the Iron Cross of Germany. In May 1881, I founded the American Association of the Red Cross (chartered in 1893), along with a group of well-respected colleagues. I held the office of president and was a pioneer of large-scale disaster relief for the next 23 years. During those years, I supervised relief work in 21 disasters, including the Johnstown, Pennsylvania, flood (1889), the Spanish-American War (1898), and the Galveston, Texas flood (1900).

My life of public service began on December 25, 1821, in North Oxford, Massachusetts. I was educated at home by my four brothers and sisters; my education plunged me into an early teaching career at local schools in New Jersey. After additional education, I moved to Bordentown, New Jersey, and established the state's first successful free school. Two years later (1854), I moved to Washington, DC, to become a clerk for the United States Patent Office. But I resigned with the outbreak of the Civil War, fulfilling my inner need to help others. After a life-long commitment to the cause, I died on April 12, 1912, in Glen Echo, Maryland.

WHO AM I?

1. My life of public service began on December 25, 1821, in North Oxford, Massachusetts.
2. In Bordentown, New Jersey, I established the state's first free school.
3. I moved to Washington, DC, to become a clerk in the United States Patent Office, but I resigned with the outbreak of the Civil War.
4. During the Civil War, I delivered supplies and offered aid to wounded soldiers. This aid earned me the names of "Angel of the Battlefield" and the "Yankee Florence Nightingale."
5. In May 1881, I founded the American Red Cross and held the office of president for the next 23 years. During those years, I supervised relief work in 21 disasters, including the Johnstown, Pennsylvania, flood (1889), the Spanish-American War (1898), and the Galveston, Texas, flood (1900).

I was commissioned by George Washington, George Ross, and Robert Morris to sew the "Stars and Stripes," which would become the first American flag. On May 29, 1777, the Pennsylvania State Navy Board ordered that I receive the payment of 14/12/2 francs for my services of making flags for the state. That same year in June (June 14, 1777), the "Stars and Stripes" was adopted as our national flag by a resolution issued by the Continental Congress.

My life began on January 1, 1752, in Philadelphia, Pennsylvania. At an early age my skill for needlework emerged while attending the Friends' School on South Fourth Street. I opened an upholstery shop with my husband (also a soldier in the militia), but on January 21, 1776, he was killed while on patrol. The times were hard, but still I continued the business on my own. I remarried two more times, but with the same result. Nineteen years (January 30, 1836) after my third husband's death, I died in Philadelphia, Pennsylvania.

WHO AM I?

1. I was born on January 1, 1752, in Philadelphia, Pennsylvania.
2. I opened an upholstery shop with my husband, but was forced to run the business by myself when he was killed on January 21, 1776.
3. On January 30, 1836, in Philadelphia, Pennsylvania, I died.
4. While attending the Friends' School, my skill for needlework emerged.
5. I was commissioned by George Washington, George Ross, and Robert Morris to sew the "Stars and Stripes." On June 14, 1777, the "Stars and Stripes" was adopted as our national flag by a resolution issued by the Continental Congress.

5

For 50 years I worked for better living conditions and treatment of the mentally ill and prisoners. My crusade began in Massachusetts, but eventually spread to every state east of the Rockies. In 1841, while teaching a Sunday School class in the East Cambridge (Massachusetts) House of Corrections, my eyes were opened to the poor living conditions, which were compounded by mixing prisoners with the mentally ill. In 1848, I traveled to Washington, DC, to lobby for the passage of a bill that would have set aside land for the mentally ill. The bill past both houses, but President Franklin Pierce vetoed it in 1854. Still I was able to bring a better understanding of the mentally ill to our nation, which established 32 new hospitals in 15 states and the District of Columbia, and prompted six other asylums to enlarge their facilities.

My life began on April 4, 1802, in Hampden, Maine. I was only 14 when I began teaching school. Five years later, I opened an all girls school in the Dix Mansion owned by my grandmother. I taught there for 14 years until poor health forced me to retire. With improved health, I began working for the rights of the mentally ill. When the Civil War broke out in 1861, I was appointed Superintendent of Army Nurses on June 10, 1861. In 1881 at the age of 79, I retired and lived at the New Jersey State Hospital (first mental hospital built due to my crusade). I died there on July 17, 1887, of arteriosclerosis.

WHO AM I?

1. My life began on April 4, 1802, in Hampden, Maine.
2. I was just 14 when I began teaching school.
3. When the Civil War broke out in 1861, I was appointed Superintendent of Army Nurses on June 10.
4. In 1841, while teaching a Sunday School class in the East Cambridge (Massachusetts) House of Corrections, my eyes were opened to the poor living conditions of the prisoners.
5. I labored 50 years to improve the living conditions and treatment of prisoners and the mentally ill. Through my efforts 32 new hospitals in 15 states and the District of Columbia were built, and six other asylums were enlarged.

6

In September 1918, I found out that my husband was having an affair with my social secretary, Lucy Page Mercer. After that I took an added interest in my husband's gaining the presidency. I was able to get equal pay for women in the NRA codes, establish work projects for the unemployed, convince the AAA to use surplus farm goods to feed the hungry, and establish "Arthurdale," a community for unemployed coal miners. After my husband's death, President Truman appointed me as a delegate to the United Nations in December 1945. As a member of the U.N.'s Human Rights Commission, I was instrumental in drafting a Universal Declaration of Human Rights that was later adopted by the U.N.'s General Assembly. When Kennedy became President, he made me a delegate once again, appointed me to the Peace Corps' Advisory Board, and asked me to be chairwoman of the President's Commission on the Status of Women.

My life began on October 11, 1884, in New York City, New York. I was a painfully shy, insecure child, who never thought much about politics. By the time I was 10, both my parents had died and I went to live with my grandmother. There I learned French, rode horses, and did an enormous amount of reading and writing on my own. I was an overachiever, always trying to win the approval of my grandmother and those in authority. When I was 15, my grandmother sent me to England to study at Allenwood. There I learned self-discipline and creative thinking. During World War I, I served my country in the Red Cross, serving snacks and knitting clothing for servicemen. I further served my country from 1942 to 1944, as I traveled to American bases overseas to boost the morale of troops under the code name "Rover." My service to my country ended on November 7, 1962 (at the age of 78), in New York City, New York.

WHO AM I?

1. I was born on October 11, 1884, in New York City, New York.
2. When I was 15, my grandmother sent me to England to study at Allenwood.
3. During World War I, I served my country in the Red Cross, serving snacks and knitting clothing for servicemen.
4. From 1942 to 1944, I traveled to American bases overseas to boost the morale of troops under the code name "Rover."

5. When I found out that my husband was having an affair with my social secretary, Lucy Page Mercer, I took an added interest in my husband's life and later in his presidency.

7   In 1889, I began my crusade against what I felt was the greatest evil of all — alcohol. Three years later, I founded a local branch of the Women's Christian Temperance Union to combat illegal liquor sales (Kansas Prohibition Amendment passed in 1880). It was apparent that nothing was going to be done until women were given the right to vote, so I began supporting the women's rights movement. In 1899, with the help of a few women supporters, I began taking action against illegal saloons to shut them down. On June 6, 1900, I single-handedly closed down three saloons by destroying them with bricks, rocks, and even my famed "hatchet."

I drew national attention in December of that same year, when I destroyed Wichita's Hotel Carey saloon, for which I was given a two week jail sentence.

My life began on November 25, 1846, in rural Garrard County, Kentucky. In 1867, I married a physician, Charles Gloyd; our marriage produced a daughter.

After my husband's death I attended the normal school in Warrensburg, Missouri to become a school teacher. Twelve years later, I began speaking out against the evils of alcohol, which killed my first husband and was destroying our daughter Charlien. My crusade lasted about two years (1901), then my audience began to fade as I was out on the lecture tour trying to pay off my legal fees.

In 1903 (my last public appearance), I was in the play, "Hatchetation," where I was featured in a scene that called for me to smash up the saloon. I died on June 9, 1911, in Leavenworth, Kansas, at the age of 64.

WHO AM I?

1. My life began on November 25, 1846, in rural Garrard County, Kentucky.
2. After my first husband's death, I attended the normal school in Warrensburg, Missouri, to become a school teacher.
3. In 1903, I appeared in the play, "Hatchetation," where I was featured in a scene that called for me to smash up a saloon.
4. In 1889, I began my crusade against the greatest evil of all—alcohol. Three years later, I founded a local branch of the Women's Christian Temperance Union to combat illegal liquor sales in Kansas.
5. On June 6, 1900, I single-handedly closed down three saloons by destroying them with bricks, rocks, and even my famed "hatchet." I drew national attention in December of that same year when I destroyed Wichita's Hotel Carey saloon, for which I received a two week jail sentence.

8

During the Revolutionary War (June 28, 1778) at the Battle of Monmouth, I carried water from a nearby spring to refresh my husband and the other artillerymen. When my husband, John C. Hays, was wounded while loading his cannon, I jumped behind the cannon and fired upon the enemy throughout the rest of the battle. I also served as a cook, nurse, and laundress for the soldiers. It was for my efforts on the battlefield delivering water that I gained my famous nickname.

I was born Mary Ludwig on October 13, 1750, near Trenton, New Jersey. Later, I went to work as a house servant in Carlisle, Pennsylvania. There I met and married my first husband in 1769. After the Revolutionary War my husband and I returned to Carlisle for the next 20 years until his death. In 1822, the Pennsylvania Legislature awarded me an annual $40 pension for the rest of my life, because I was a widow of a Revolutionary War soldier. I died on January 22, 1832, in Carlisle, Pennsylvania.

WHO AM I?

1. I was born Mary Ludwig on October 13, 1750, near Trenton, New Jersey.
2. Later, I went to work as a house servant in Carlisle, Pennsylvania. There I met and married my first husband in 1769.
3. In 1822, the Pennsylvania Legislature awarded me an annual $40 pension for the rest of my life. I died on January 22, 1832, in Carlisle, Pennsylvania.
4. When my husband, John C. Hays, was wounded while loading his cannon (Revolutionary War), I jumped behind the cannon and fired upon the enemy throughout the rest of the battle.
5. During the Revolutionary War (June 28, 1778) at the Battle of Monmouth, I carried water from a nearby spring to refresh my husband and the other artillerymen. For my efforts, I gained my famous nickname.

9

Anne Mansfield Sullivan taught me how to spell by slowly making letters into my hand. As I was able to spell a few words, she began giving me pieces of cardboard with Braille letters (raised dots) on them. In 1890, I learned to speak with the help of Miss

Sarah Fuller, principal of the Horace Mann School. Six years later, with the help of my dear friend Miss Sullivan, I entered the Cambridge School for Young Ladies.

Miss Sullivan also helped me three years later, when I took my final exams to get into Radcliffe College, which I passed. In 1924, I devoted the rest of my life to raising funds and public interest to the problems encountered by the physically handicapped for the American Foundation for the Blind.

My life began on a bright note on June 27, 1880, in Tuscumbia, Alabama, but it soon darkened when an illness, acute congestion of the brain and stomach, stripped me of my sight, hearing, and speech. My world began to brighten when Miss Sullivan came into my life, when I was almost seven years old. She encouraged me to go to the Perkins Institute for the Blind, where I learned the manual alphabet.

In 1894, I went to the Wright-Humason School for the Deaf (New York City). I later went on to college, became a suffragette, went on the lecture tour, wrote some books, made a movie based on my life, and for two years appeared on the vaudeville stage. I died on June 1, 1968, in Westport, Connecticut.

WHO AM I?

1. My life began on June 27, 1880, in Tuscumbia, Alabama.
2. In 1890, I learned to speak with the help of Miss Sarah Fuller, principal of the Horace Mann School.
3. In 1924, I devoted the rest of my life to raising funds for the American Foundation for the Blind.
4. When I was 19 months old, acute congestion of the brain and stomach stripped me of my sight, hearing, and speech.
5. Miss (Anne Mansfield) Sullivan taught me how to spell by slowly making letters in my hand.

10 On June 18, 1983, at 7:33 a.m. EST, the space shuttle *Challenger* rose off the rocket pad at Cape Canaveral, Florida, making me the first American women in space. Almost a year earlier, Navy Captain Robert L. Crippen (commander of the shuttle mission) had chosen me for his crew. I served as a mission specialist and flight engineer for that seventh shuttle mission, in which we tested a robot arm in space for the very first time. Six days later, we landed at Edwards Air Force Base in California.

I was born on May 26, 1951, in Encino, California. At the age of ten, I began playing tennis under the watchful eye of former U.S. Open star, Alice Marble. Eventually, I had a national ranking of 18th, which won me a partial scholarship to the Westlake School for Girls. There I discovered science, which would soon sideline my tennis career. After graduating from Stanford University with a double major in physics and English literature in 1973, I entered graduate school in astrophysics. While working on my doctoral dissertation, I applied to the National Aeronautics & Space Administration (NASA). I became one of the their 208 finalists in October 1977. By January 1978, I was a member of the new astronaut class. After receiving my Ph.D., I traveled to the Johnson Space Center to begin my intensive astronaut training with 29 men and 5 other women.

WHO AM I?

1. I was born on May 26, 1951, in Encino, California.
2. At the age of ten, I began playing tennis under the watchful eye of former U.S. Open star, Alice Marble.
3. After graduating from Stanford University with a double major in physics and English literature in 1973, I entered graduate school in astrophysics.
4. While working on my doctoral dissertation, I applied to the National Aeronautics & Space Administration (NASA).
5. On June 18, 1983, at 7:33 a.m. EST, the space shuttle *Challenger* rose off the rocket pad in Cape Canaveral, Florida, making me the first American woman in space.

11

My lavish dinner parties made me one of the most popular first ladies. I did not have much interest in politics, but I loved to entertain those who did. Often I would wear beautiful, colorful gowns to entertain at fancy dinner parties, balls, and receptions. I served as a part-time hostess for Thomas Jefferson for eight years and a full-time hostess for eight years when my husband took office (March 1809). On August 24, 1814, I fled Washington, DC (as the British were approaching), with important papers, books, silver, and a portrait of George Washington painted by Gilbert Stuart loaded into a wagon.

I was born Dorothea Payne on May 20, 1768, in Guilford County, North Carolina. My mother taught me to cook and sew; my grandmother taught me about fine foods and fabrics. Entertaining was a part of life, but after my second marriage (first husband, John Todd, died during the yellow fever epidemic) it became an even larger part. With my husband's position as Secretary of State for Jefferson's presidency, I entertained at diplomatic dinners, serving only American dishes. My flair for entertaining continued well after my husband retired to Montpelier after his presidency. I entertained for the last time on July 12, 1849, in Orange County, Virginia, at the age of 81.

WHO AM I?

1. I was born Dorothea Payne on May 20, 1768, in Guilford County, North Carolina.

2. My mother taught me to cook and sew; my grandmother taught me about fine foods and fabrics.

3. With my husband's position as Secretary of State for Jefferson's presidency, I entertained at diplomatic dinners, serving only American dishes.

4. I served as a part-time hostess for President Thomas Jefferson for his eight years in office.

5. My lavish dinner parties made me one of the most popular first ladies (served for eight years, beginning in March 1809). On August 24, 1814, I fled Washington, DC (as the British were approaching), with important papers, books, silver, and a portrait of George Washington painted by Gilbert Stuart loaded into a wagon.

12	On September 25, 1981, I was sworn in as the first woman member of the United States Supreme Court. I was nominated to the high court by President Ronald Reagan on July 7, 1981, to replace the retiring Potter Stewart. The United States Senate con-

firmed my nomination with a vote of 99 to 0, which made me the 102nd member of the court and Associate Justice of the Supreme Court. I remain in this capacity today. Earlier in my career, I had another first as a woman. In 1973, I became the first woman senate majority leader in Arizona and the country.

My life began on March 26, 1930, in El Paso, Texas. My school days were spent with my grandmother back in El Paso. Instead of attending the rural schools in Arizona, I attended a private girls school (Radford School). I graduated from Austin High School at the age of 16, then moved on to Stanford where I majored in economics. I received my B.A. in 1950 and my L.L.B. in 1952. After college a Los Angeles firm offered me a job as a legal secretary, which I strongly rejected. Later, I worked as a deputy attorney for San Mateo County, California, then served as a civilian lawyer for the Quartermaster Corps in Frankfurt, West Germany, while my husband was in the service. Then I began climbing the ladder, first as an assistant attorney general of Arizona (1965–1968), then as a state senator for five years (1969–1974), then as a judge on the superior court in Arizona (1974), and on the Court of Appeals (1979), the position I held when I was nominated to my present position.

WHO AM I?

1. I was born on March 26, 1930, in El Paso, Texas.
2. I graduated from Austin High School at the age of 16.
3. At Stanford I majored in economics, receiving my B.A. in 1950 and my L.L.B. in 1952.
4. I began climbing the ladder, first as an assistant attorney general of Arizona (1965–1968), then as a state senator for five years (1969–1974), then as a judge on the superior court in Arizona (1974), and on the Court of Appeals (1979).
5. On September 25, 1981, I was sworn in as the first woman member of the United States Supreme Court. I was nominated to the high court by President Ronald Reagan on July 7, 1981, to replace the retiring Potter Stewart.

Chapter Three
African Americans

 1

Through my years as a slave, I committed myself to telling others about the injustices of slavery through my lectures and writings. As my skills as a speaker grew, so did my popularity at antislavery meetings. In August 1845, I traveled to England to conduct a series of lectures on antislavery and reform.

When I returned to the United States two years later, I published my weekly abolitionist newspaper, the *North Star* (Rochester, New York) to showcase my thoughts and views on the welfare of blacks in the United States. I told my story in two books: *The Heroic Slave* (1853) and *My Bondage and Freedom* (1855). I died on February 20, 1895, in Washington, DC.

I was born on February 7, 1817, in Tuckahoe, Maryland (on the Eastern Shore). As a young boy, I was sent to work for the Hugh Auld family in Baltimore. Here I enjoyed many privileges that I had been denied at Colonel Edward Lloyd's plantation. I was able to develop my mind at the East Baltimore Mental Improvement Society, where I met several free blacks. It was from one of these new friends that I borrowed free papers and boarded the train to New York. I went by the name of Frederick Augustus Washington Bailey until I moved to Massachusetts. With the help of my British friends, I purchased my freedom from the Auld family for $700.

WHO AM I?

1. I was born on February 7, 1817, on a plantation in Tuckahoe, Maryland (on the Eastern Shore).

2. As a boy, I was sent to work for the Hugh Auld family in Baltimore. Here I enjoyed many privileges that I was denied at Colonel Edward Lloyd's plantation. With the help of my British friends, I purchased my freedom from the Auld family for $700.

3. I told my story in two books: *The Heroic Slave* (1853) and *My Bondage and Freedom* (1855).

4. Through my years as a slave, I committed myself to telling others about the injustices of slavery through my lectures and writings. To showcase my thoughts and views on the welfare of blacks in the United States, I published my weekly abolitionist newspaper, the *North Star* (Rochester, New York).

5. I went by the name of Frederick Augustus Washington Bailey until I moved to Massachusetts.

2

Through the Underground Railroad I was able to lead more than 300 slaves to freedom in the North. This number included my parents, who I brought to freedom in 1857. I made 20 trips to the South, with the help of some Quakers who were committed to the cause. These trips were always dangerous, but I never let the danger stop my efforts. Between my trips to the South, I worked as a freelance writer for the National Anti-Slavery Standard in New York City, as a speaker at antislavery meetings in Boston, and as a cook. During the Civil War, I served as a nurse, cook, scout, and spy for the Union Army.

I was born into slavery as Araminta in 1826 on a plantation in Dorchester County, Maryland. Early on I worked as a field hand on the plantation. When I was six, my master Edward Brodas hired me out to Mrs. James Cook for a small monthly fee. In 1844, my master forced me to marry a fellow slave to produce offspring. Five years later, I fled to freedom in the North without my husband. During my exploits, I met John Brown who later became a friend. After the Civil War I moved to Auburn, New York, where my parents lived. I died there on March 10, 1913.

WHO AM I?

1. I was born into slavery as Araminta in 1826 on a plantation in Dorchester County, Maryland.
2. When I was six, my master Edward Brodas hired me out to Mrs. James Cook for a small monthly fee.
3. During the Civil War, I served as a nurse, cook, scout, and spy for the Union Army.
4. Between my trips to the South, I worked as a freelance writer for the National Anti-Slavery Standard in New York City, as a speaker at anti-slavery meetings in Boston, and as a cook.
5. Through the Underground Railroad I was able to lead more than 300 slaves to freedom in the North. I made 20 trips to the South, with the help of some Quakers who were committed to the cause.

3

On August 28, 1963, my March on Washington brought more than 200,000 marchers (of all races) together at the Lincoln Memorial to demand equal rights for all Americans. In 1964, I was given the Nobel Prize for Peace for my use of nonviolent resistance as a means of protest. The next year (March 21, 1965), I organized my famous Freedom March that brought together over 100,000 people to march from Selma, Alabama to the state capital in Montgomery, to bring national attention to the fact that we were in need of a federal voting rights law. As a result of our efforts, the Voting Rights Act of 1965 was passed. Three years later, on April 4, 1968, I was gunned down by an assassin on the balcony of the Lorraine Motel (Memphis, Tennessee).

I was born with the given name Michael on January 15 (recognized as a holiday), 1929, in Atlanta, Georgia. While attending Morehouse College (freshman at 15), I was ordained a Baptist minister. After graduation I attended the Crozer Theological Seminary (Chester, Pennsylvania), where I met with the teachings of Mahatma Gandhi. His teachings were the biggest influence on my life. In 1951, I went to Boston University's graduate school to earn my Ph.D. (spring of 1955). A year after my marriage to Coretta Scott (June 18, 1953), I became a pastor of the Dexter Avenue Baptist Church (Montgomery, Alabama). My sermons soon touched a nation, and my dream encouraged others to speak out for civil rights.

WHO AM I?

1. I was born on January 15, 1929, in Atlanta, Georgia.
2. At the Crozer Theological Seminary (Chester, Pennsylvania), I met with the teachings of Mahatma Gandhi. His teachings were the biggest influence on my life.
3. While attending Morehouse College (freshman at 15), I was ordained a Baptist minister.
4. On August 28, 1963, my March on Washington brought more than 200,000 marchers (of all races) together at the Lincoln Memorial to demand equal rights for all Americans. In 1964, I was given the Nobel Prize for Peace for my use of nonviolent resistance as a means of protest.
5. On March 21, 1965, I organized my famous Freedom March that brought together over 100,000 people to march from Selma, Alabama, to the state capital in Montgomery, to bring attention to the fact that we were in need of a federal voting rights law. As a result of our efforts, the Voting Rights Act of 1965 was passed.

4 Where I grew up, there were no schools for black children, so I decided to do something about it. I started my own school in Georgia, then I built a new school called the Daytona Educational and Industrial Training School for children whose fathers worked on the railroad. It became one of the first black schools in the state of Florida to offer a high school curriculum. It later changed names and was known as the Bethune-Cookman College. I served as its president and instated several progams not previously offered to blacks: adult education classes to prepare students to become voters, library services for students who were not allowed in public libraries, and a hospital on campus for students who were not allowed in the all-white hospitals in Daytona. For my efforts with young people, President Franklin D. Roosevelt appointed me

to the National Youth Administration's advisory board. I died on May 18, 1955 (at the age of 79), in Daytona Beach, Florida.

I was born free on July 10, 1875, in Mayesville (Sumter County), South Carolina. My mother and father were born into slavery, and my great, great-grandfather was an African chieftain. At a young age, I knew I wanted to be a teacher and help my own people. I began helping my teacher, Miss Wilson, with the other children. She recommended me for a scholarship to Scotia, which I attended for seven years. After graduation I went to the Moody Bible Institute for two years. I felt ready to teach after that, so I returned to my hometown. Later, I taught at the Haines Normal and Industrial Institute for three years. Then I knew it was time to strike out on my own, with the help of some knowledge from the Kendal Institute.

WHO AM I?

1. I was born free on July 10, 1875, in Mayesville (Sumter County), South Carolina.
2. My mother and father were born into slavery, and my great, great-grandfather was an African chieftain.
3. I attended the Moody Bible Institute for two years. Later, I taught at the Haines Normal and Industrial Institute for three years.
4. For my efforts with young people, President Franklin D. Roosevelt appointed me to the National Youth Administration's advisory board.
5. I built a new school called the Daytona Educational and Industrial Training School for children whose fathers worked on the railroad. It became one of the first black schools in the state of Florida to offer a high school curriculum.

5

In 1895, I became the first black to earn a Ph.D. from Harvard. Ten years later, I organized the Niagara Movement in Ontario, Canada, which was the first black protest movement. When the National Association for the Advancement of Colored People (NAACP) was founded on May 12, 1910, I became the director of publication and research for their magazine, *The Crisis*. I also served as editor and writer for the magazine for 26 years. In 1961 I went to live in Ghana to complete my work on the *Encyclopedia Africana*. It was here that I died on August 27, 1963 (Accra, Ghana).

I was born on February 23, 1868, in Great Barrington, Massachusetts. My flair for writing emerged in high school as a local correspondent for my school's newspaper (the Springfield *Republican*). This interest in writing continued to grow in college, where I was editor of the Fisk University *Herald*. Here I also developed my skills as a public speaker. Then I began putting my thoughts into books, including *The Negro* (1915), *Black Reconstruction* (1939), *Dusk of Dawn* (1940), and *Black Folk Then and Now* (1940).

WHO AM I?

1. I was born on February 23, 1868, in Great Barrington, Massachusetts.

2. My flair for writing emerged in high school as a local correspondent for my school's newspaper (the Springfield *Republican*). This interest in writing continued to grow in college, where I was editor of the Fisk University *Herald*.
3. In 1895 I became the first black to earn a Ph.D. from Harvard.
4. Then I began putting my thoughts into books, including *The Negro* (1915), *Black Reconstruction* (1939), *Dusk of Dawn* (1940), and *Black Folk Then and Now* (1940).
5. In 1910, I organized the Niagara Movement in Ontario, Canada, which was the first black protest movement. When the NAACP was founded on May 12th of that same year, I became the director of publication and research for their magazine, *The Crisis*.

6

The Montgomery boycott of city buses was waged because of my actions taken on the evening of December 1, 1955. I was very tired that evening, so I sat near the front of the bus in the "white section." You see, the first four rows of the bus were reserved for "whites only," and the next two or three rows after that could be used by blacks if there were no whites present. I was sitting in one of these seats as the bus began to fill up. When the bus driver noticed that I was sitting while a white passenger was forced to stand, he ordered me out of the seat. I did not move, so I was arrested and jailed.

I was born on February 4, 1913, in Tuskegee, Alabama. After college I became a member of the NAACP and worked as one of their youth advisors. To help support my family, I worked as a seamstress at a local department store (Fair Department Store) in Montgomery. Under the pressure of the boycott, I was fired from my job and my husband became very ill. We moved to Detroit, Michigan, where I worked as a dressmaker, youth advisor, and staff assistant to United States Representative John Conyers.

WHO AM I?

1. I was born on February 4, 1913, in Tuskegee, Alabama.
2. To help support my family I worked as a seamstress at a local department store (Fair Department Store) in Montgomery.

3. We moved to Detroit, Michigan, where I worked as a dressmaker, youth advisor, and staff assistant to United States Representative John Conyers.
4. After college I became a member of the NAACP and worked as one of their youth advisors.
5. The Montgomery boycott of city buses was waged because of my actions taken on the evening of December 1, 1955. That day I refused to move out of my seat that was generally reserved for whites. I was arrested and jailed for my actions, but it was well worth it to end segregation on buses.

7 In 1881, General Samuel C. Armstrong chose me as the first principal of the Tuskegee Institute, a normal and agricultural school for blacks in Tuskegee, Alabama. I was very successful at fundraising and promoting the school; taking it from a school with only 40 students to a nationally recognized, leading school for blacks. In 1895, I gained more national recognition for my "Atlanta Compromise" speech on race relations. I died on November 14, 1915, in Tuskegee, Alabama, totally exhausted from my work. In 1945, I was elected to the Hall of Fame for Great Americans.

I was born a slave on April 5, 1856, on the James Burroughs plantation in Franklin County, Virginia. As a child I thirsted for knowledge, and I began to quench that thirst when I attended the Hampton Normal and Agricultural Institute (1872) in Virginia. I studied there for three years and paid for my tuition and expenses by working as a janitor. After teaching for two years in my hometown, I returned to school at the Wayland Seminary (1878–1879) in Washington, DC. Then I joined the faculty at Hampton to teach a pilot program for Native Americans, where I impressed General Samuel C. Armstrong, who would soon ask me to lead his newly founded normal school for blacks.

WHO AM I?

1. I was born a slave on April 5, 1856, on the James Burroughs plantation in Franklin County, Virginia.
2. I attended the Hampton Normal and Agricultural Institute in Virginia.

I studied there for three years and paid for my tuition and expenses by working as a janitor.

3. In 1895, I gained national recognition for my "Atlanta Compromise" speech on racial relations.

4. I died on November 14, 1915, in Tuskegee, Alabama, totally exhausted from my work. In 1945, I was elected to the Hall of Fame for Great Americans.

5. In 1881, General Samuel C. Armstrong chose me as the first principal of the Tuskegee Institute, a normal and agricultural school for blacks in Tuskegee, Alabama. I took the school from having only 40 students to being a nationally recognized, leading school for blacks.

8 In 1967, I became the first black member of the United States Supreme Court (nominated by President Lyndon B. Johnson). Two years earlier, President Johnson had appointed me United States Solicitor General (first black to hold that office). As an NAACP lawyer I tried 32 major cases, one of which was the *Brown v. Board of Education* (1954) case. In that court decision, the United States Supreme court unanimously voted that racial segregation in public schools was unconstitutional because it denied blacks their rights under the 14th Amendment. This was a ringing victory for the civil rights movement. In 1961, my climb to higher office began when President John F. Kennedy nominated me to the United States Court of Appeals (took office in 1962).

I was born on July 2, 1908, in Baltimore, Maryland. My great-grandfather had been a slave, which encouraged me to fight against the injustices that he had suffered. I worked diligently to put myself through college, first earning a degree at Lincoln University (1930) and then a law degree from Howard University (1933). I was admitted to the bar in 1933 and began my concentration in the area of civil rights. While in private practice in Baltimore, I began trying cases for the NAACP. Two years later, they made me their Head of Legal Services. I worked in the organization for 23 years, accumulating a record of 29 wins, 3 losses.

WHO AM I?

1. I was born on July 2, 1908, in Baltimore, Maryland.

2. I earned my law degree from Howard University (1933) and was admitted to the bar that same year.
3. In 1961, President John F. Kennedy nominated me to the United States Court of Appeals (took office in 1962).
4. As an NAACP lawyer I tried 32 major cases, one of which was the *Brown v. Board of Education* (1954) case.

5. In 1967, I became the first black member of the United States Supreme Court (nominated by President Lyndon B. Johnson).

9 In 1843, I began speaking out against slavery as an evangelist and preacher in New York City. I became a featured speaker (often rivaling Frederick Douglass) at abolitionist crusades, where I also began speaking out for women's rights. Angry mobs and law enforcement officers often tried to silence me, but this aggression only spurred me on to work harder. For my efforts, President Abraham Lincoln appointed me counselor to the freedman at the nation's capital. After the Civil War I worked with the Freedman's Bureau to provide education and employment for former slaves. I also continued speaking out on various black causes. I died on November 26, 1883, in Battle Creek, Michigan.

My life began as a slave named Isabella Van Wagener around 1797 in Ulster County, New York. I was sold at a very young age and forced to serve several masters, one of whom was the father of my five children; in an unprecedented court case, I was able to rescue one of my children from slavery. In 1827, the New York State Emancipation Act gave me my freedom and I moved to New York. Sixteen years later, I adopted a new name and began traveling the countryside proclaiming truth and speaking out against injustices as my ordination from God.

WHO AM I?

1. My life began as a slave named Isabella Van Wagener around 1797 in Ulster County, New York.
2. In 1827, the New York State Emancipation Act gave me my freedom and I moved to New York.
3. President Abraham Lincoln appointed me counselor to the freedman at the nation's capital.
4. After the Civil War I worked with the Freedman's Bureau to provide education and employment for former slaves.
5. In 1843, I adopted a new name and began traveling the countryside proclaiming truth and speaking out against slavery as an evangelist and preacher in New York City.

Betsy Graves

| 10 | In 1896, I went to Tuskegee Institute at Booker T. Washington's insistence. Here I taught the values of crop rotation, multi-crop farming, and the use of fertilizers. I also began working on my synthetic products. As a synthetic chemist, I synthesized 125 dif- |

ferent products from sweet potatoes and more than 300 different products from peanuts ("goobers"). I also developed thousands of useful products from such things as cotton, wild plums, cowpeas, Alabama clay, waste material, and many other indigenous plants. In 1923, I was honored with the Spingarn Medal for my contributions to my race.

I was born on January 5, 1864, in Diamond Grove, Missouri. As a small child, I loved plants and was blessed with the ability to grow anything. I transplanted flowers and plants from nearby fields and woods, which multiplied under my tender loving care. My mother's garden was my playground and the envy of our neighborhood. At college (Iowa State), I majored in botany and agricultural chemistry and received my B.A. in 1894. After graduation I joined the faculty at Iowa State and taught bacterial botany and agriculture, while working on my master's.

WHO AM I?

1. I was born on January 5, 1864, in Diamond Grove, Missouri.
2. In 1923, I was honored with the Spingarn Medal for my contributions to my race.
3. As a small child, I loved plants and was blessed with the ability to grow anything. My mother's garden was my playground and the envy of our neighborhood.
4. At college (Iowa State), I majored in botany and agricultural chemistry and received my B.A. in 1894.
5. In 1896, I went to teach at Tuskegee Institute at Booker T. Washington's insistence. Here I began working on my synthetic products. I synthesized 125 different products from sweet potatoes and more than 300 different products from peanuts ("goobers").

After Rosa Parks' arrest in Montgomery for refusing to give up her seat for a white passenger, Dr. King and I organized a boycott of city buses (the boycott lasted more than a year). I came up with the idea of a boycott, but Dr. King was the sparkplug, the leader. In 1957, we paired up again to organize the Southern Christian Leadership Conference (SCLC); I served as the secretary-treasurer while Dr. King was the president. Through the SCLC we organized efforts to get blacks out to vote, sit-ins to help the cause, and often ended up in jail together for speaking out on our beliefs.

I was born on March 11, 1926, on the family farm in Linden, Alabama.

My grandfather was a slave, so I knew first hand the injustices that he had suffered. I also knew of the injustices of growing up black in a white America. As a child I loved to read and study, so it was not a surprise that I went on to college and later became an ordained Baptist minister. It was as pastor of a Baptist church that I met my dear friend Dr. Martin Luther King, Jr., who felt one day that I should be his successor. After Dr. King's death, I built "Resurrection City, U.S.A." (Washington, DC), to bring attention to the plight of African Americans. The police tore down the city and gave me 20 days in jail, but they could never destroy the dream.

WHO AM I?

1. I was born on March 11, 1926, in Linden, Alabama.
2. My grandfather was a slave, so I knew first hand the injustices that he had suffered.
3. After Dr. Martin Luther King's death, I built "Resurrection City, U.S.A." in Washington, DC.
4. In 1957, I paired up with Dr. King to organize the Southern Christian Leadership Conference (SCLC).
5. After Rosa Parks' arrest in Montgomery for refusing to give up her seat to a white passenger, Dr. King and I organized a boycott of city buses (the boycott lasted more than a year).

12

In 1971, I founded the Chicago-based Operation PUSH (People United to Save Humanity), which later changed its name to People United to Serve Humanity. PUSH encouraged local businesses to hire more blacks and promote them on the basis of merit. It also encouraged businesses to work with black-owned businesses to help promote them in the community. In 1983, I declared my candidacy for the Democratic Presidential nomination after launching a black, national voter-registration drive. The following year, I finished a respectable third (behind former Vice President Walter Mondale and Senator Gary Hart) in a large field of contenders in the Democratic primary.

I was born on October 8, 1941, in Greenville, South Carolina. My first involvement with the civil rights movement and the economic problems (specifically labor) that plague African Americans began while attending the University of Illinois (1959–1960) and the North Carolina Agricultural and Technical College (received my B.A. in 1964). After graduation I entered the Chicago Theological Seminary for postgraduate studies. In 1968, I became an ordained Baptist minister. Earlier in 1967, I was named to Operation Breadbasket (which I helped found) by the Southern Christian Leadership Conference (SCLC). In December 1983, I worked for the release of an United States Navy flier captured in Syria.

WHO AM I?

1. My life began on October 8, 1941, in Greenville, South Carolina.
2. After postgraduate studies at the Chicago Theological Seminary, I became an ordained Baptist minister in 1968.
3. In 1967, I was named to Operation Breadbasket (which I helped found) by the Southern Christian Leadership Conference (SCLC).
4. Four years later, I founded the Chicago-based Operation PUSH (People United to Save Humanity), which later changed its name to People United to Serve Humanity.
5. In 1983, I declared my candidacy for the Democratic Presidential nomination after launching a black, national voter-registration drive. The following year, I finished a respectable third (behind former Vice President Walter Mondale and Senator Gary Hart) in the Democratic primary.

Chapter Four
Stars of the Silver Screen

1

My greatest success came from my title role as a saloon singer in *Diamond Lil* (1928), which I wrote and set in the "Gay Nineties." In June 1932, I left for the bright lights of Hollywood to work under contract to Paramount Pictures at $5,000 a week. I starred in a string of films, beginning with *Night After Night* (1932) and *She Done Him Wrong* (1933), which set records at the box-office. That same year, the film *I'm No Angel* (1933) surpassed my previous box office records. These films allowed me to become the highest paid actor in Hollywood ($300,000 a picture and an additional $100,000 for writing the screenplay), which made me a household name. Before coming to Hollywood, I made a name for myself on the stage with the first play I had ever written, *Sex* (debuted in April 26, 1926). The play was closed down after 375 performances and I was arrested for corrupting the morals of minors. I was found guilty in a much publicized trial and sentenced to eight days in jail.

I was born on August 17, 1892, in Brooklyn, New York. By the time I was seven, I had already begun performing in amateur talent shows with my song and dance routine. A year later, I began performing with a stock company. Three years after that I was appearing in *Little Nell the Marchioness* (1901–1904).

My success continued on stage, so I quit school at the age of 13. When I turned 14, I was already performing on the vaudeville circuit with Frank Wallace (whom I later married). On September 22, 1911, I debuted in the Broadway show, *A'la Broadway & Hello, Paris*. My appearances continued in *Sometime* (1918), in which I introduced the "shimmy" dance to New York audiences in 283 performances, *The Drag* (1926), and *The Wicked Age* (1927).

WHO AM I?

1. I was born on August 17, 1892, in Brooklyn, New York.
2. I began my career in vaudeville and was a legend in American entertainment for more than 50 years.
3. In 1926, I was jailed for eight days for corrupting the morals of minors.
4. At the age of 84, I starred in *Sextette* (1977).
5. My plays include: *Sex* (1926), *The Drag* (1926), and *Diamond Lil* (1928). I wrote the screenplays for my films: *She Done Him Wrong* (1933), *I'm No Angel* (1933), and *My Little Chickadee* (1940).

2   My film career began in 1931, with the films *Bad Sister* and *Seed*. Universal Studios thought they made a mistake when they signed me to a one-year contract, so they began loaning me out to other studios. My first important film that recognized my talent was *The Man Who Played God* (1932); with this success Warner Bros. signed me to a long-term contract. My first film for Warner Bros. was *The Rich Are Always with Us* (1932); then I played Mildred in *Of Human Bondage* (1934). I reached Hollywood stardom with my two Academy Awards for best actress in the films, *Dangerous* (1935) and *Jezebel* (1938). My box office attraction continued with such films as *Dark Victory* (1940), *The Little Foxes* (1941), *All About Eve* (1950), *What Ever Happened to Baby Jane?* (1962), and *Hush . . . Hush, Sweet Charlotte* (1965).

I was born Ruth Elizabeth (my friends call me Bess) on April 5, 1908, in Lowell, Massachusetts. At the farm school in the Berkshires, I preferred directing, building sets, and designing costumes to acting. It was not until I attended Cushing Academy that I was bitten by the acting bug. Here I acted in all the school plays and in my senior year I starred in our senior production.

My first real job came in the play *Broadway* in which I spoke one line. Then I moved on to the Cape Playhouse, where I worked mostly as an usher. I was finally given a part in a play, then returned the next two summers to appear in several other plays, including *Broken Dishes* (1929), which had an outstanding run of 178 performances. *The Man Who Played God*, *The Cabin in the Cotton*, *The Dark House*, and *Three on a Match* followed in 1932.

WHO AM I?

1. My life began on April 5, 1908, in Lowell, Massachusetts.
2. I made my Broadway debut in *Broken Dishes* (1929) and my film debut in *Bad Sister* (1931).
3. In 1934, I played Mildred in the film *Of Human Bondage*.
4. I won the Academy Award as best actress in *Dangerous* (1935) and *Jezebel* (1938).
5. My best remembered performances were in *Dark Victory* (1939), *The Little Foxes* (1941), *All About Eve* (1950), and *What Ever Happened to Baby Jane?* (1962).

3   I distinguished myself in silent films, then went on to "talkies" with minimal success. My most successful films include: *The Mothering Heart* (1913); *The Birth of a Nation* (1914); *Hearts of the World* (1918), in which I appeared with my sister Dorothy; *Broken Blossoms* (1919), which was critically acclaimed; and *The Orphans of the Storm* (1922), the last film that my sister and I made with D.W. Griffith as the director. I made my directorial debut in *Remodeling Her Husband* (1920), in which I directed my sister to a financial success at the box office. In 1922, I signed a lucrative deal with Tiffany Company, which paid me $1,250 a week plus a 15 percent gross of the picture. My first picture for them was *The White Sister* (1923). I left Tiffany in 1925 after a contract dispute, and signed with Metro-Goldwyn-Mayer. My first picture for them was *La Boheme* (1926).

I was born on October 14, 1896, in Springfield, Ohio. At an early age, my mother pushed my sister and me onto the stage. I made my stage debut in *Convict Stripes* (1902). Then the three of us went on tour in *The Little Red Schoolhouse*. By 1912, I had made my motion picture debut in *The Unseen Enemy*, in which my sister also made her debut. Then I went on tour with the production of *The Good Little Devil* (1913), where I met my dear friend Mary Pickford.

I went on to make many other films including *The Scarlet Letter* (1926) and *One Romantic Night* (1930), a "talkie" whose failure made me return to the stage. During the 1943–1944 stage season, I went on the lecture tour promoting my book *Silver Glory*.

WHO AM I?

1. I was born on October 14, 1896, in Springfield, Ohio.
2. I starred in D.W. Griffith's film, *Orphans of the Storm* (1922), with my sister Dorothy.
3. I appeared on Broadway with Mary Pickford in *A Good Little Devil* (1913).
4. My silent film credits include *The Birth of a Nation* (1914), *Broken Blossoms* (1918), and *Way Down East* (1920).
5. My "talkies" include *Duel in the Sun* (1946), *Night of the Hunter* (1955), and *The Comedians* (1967).

I won an Academy Award for the movie *It Happened One Night* (1934); it also won best picture that year. In 1937, a newspaper poll voted me the "King of Hollywood." That same year, I starred in one of the most popular movies of that year, *Test Pilot* (1937). Two years later, *Gone with the Wind* (1939) catapulted me to movie stardom. As a hot property, I followed with *Boom Town* (1940), *Honky Tonk* (1941), and *Somewhere I'll Find You* (1942). After serving in World War II in the Army Air Corps, I returned to Hollywood to make *Adventure* (1945) and *Mogambo* (1953); the latter was a hit for MGM. After turning down a more lucrative contract with MGM, I signed with 20th Century–Fox and made the films, *The Tall Man* (1955) and *The Misfits* (1961); I died in 1960 while filming *The Misfits*. My other memorable films include: *China Seas* (1935), *Mutiny on the Bounty* (1935), and *San Francisco* (1936).

My life began on February 1, 1901, in Cadiz, Ohio. In my late teens, I fell in love with acting while performing on the vaudeville stage (where I was discovered). After joining a professional acting troupe, I ended up in California with Josephine Dillion (my first wife) as my acting coach. I began as an extra in a couple of films in the mid–1920s; I had little luck, however, and moved on to the stage where my luck improved. My second try at Hollywood was not very fruitful either; my screen tests for Warners and MGM were unsuccessful. But I did not let this failure discourage me; instead it just made me work harder. It paid off when I landed a part in the play *The Painted Desert* (1931). My performance prompted MGM to offer me a contract that same year. MGM kept me busy in 1931 making six films: *Dance Fools Dance; A Free Soul,* which made me a Hollywood star;

Laughing Sinners; Sporting Blood, which gave me a starring role; *Possessed;* and *Hell's Divers,* which launched my acting career. After my wife Carole Lombard was killed in a plane crash, I began to drink heavily and developed tremors.

WHO AM I?

1. I was born on February 1, 1901, in Cadiz, Ohio.
2. At the age of 15, I gave up my plans for a medical career and became a callboy in the Akron Theater.
3. I won my only Academy Award for *It Happened One Night* (1934).
4. In 1937, a newspaper poll voted me the "King of Hollywood."
5. My most famous role was Rhett Butler in *Gone with the Wind* (1939).

5 I am best remembered for my dramatic portrayal of Norma Desmond in *Sunset Boulevard* (1950). Under Cecil B. De Mille's direction, I became one of the biggest box office attractions and movie idols of my day. I starred in six of his films, including *Male and Female* (1919) and *Don't Change Your Husband, Why Change Your Wife?* (1920). Then I went on to Paramount where I starred in *Zaza* (1923), *The Humming Bird* (1924) and *Manhandled* (1924). I turned down an $18,000 a week contract with Paramount to start my own production company (closed in 1932), with the help of my dear friend Joseph P. Kennedy. My film career blossomed, and I made several more films, including *The Loves of Sonya* (1927), *Sadie Thompson* (1928), *Indiscreet* (1931), and *Father Takes a Wife* (1941).

My life began on March 27, 1899, in Chicago, Illinois; my father called me Glory. As a child, I appeared in school plays and had hopes of becoming a great singer. At the age of 14, while touring the Essanay Studio (Chicago), I was cast as an extra in two films, *Elvira Farina* (1913) and *The Meal Ticket* (1913). Then I played the lead in the musical *The American Girl* before going to Hollywood in 1916. There I appeared in several Mack Sennett comedies, including *The Nick of Time Baby, Teddy at the Throttle,* and *The Pullman Bride,* all between 1913 and 1914. I soon moved on to dramatic roles at Triangle, such as *Everywoman's Husband* (1918) and *Her Decision* (1918). By 1948, I had my own television show (the first Holly-

wood star to do so). The curtain went down on my career for the last time on April 4, 1983, in New York City, New York.

WHO AM I?

1. I starred in Cecil B. De Mille's *Don't Change Your Husband, Why Change Your Wife?* (1920).
2. I formed my own production company in 1927 and made the film *Sadie Thompson* in 1928.
3. I appeared in the film *Airport* (1975) and frequently on television until my death on April 4, 1983, in New York City.

4. I made a brilliant comeback in 1950 with the film *Sunset Boulevard*.
5. I was born Josephine Swenson on March 27, 1899, in Chicago, Illinois.

My successful film career includes four Academy Awards as best actress; 1934 for *Morning Glory* (1933), 1968 for *Guess Who's Coming to Dinner?* (1967), 1969 for *The Lion in Winter* (1968), and 1982 for *On Golden Pond* (1981). I appeared with my good friend Spencer Tracy in nine films, including *Woman of the Year* (1942), *Pat and Mike* (1952), and *The African Queen* (1951). My other successful roles include the films *Little Women* (1933), *Alice Adams* (1935), and *The Philadelphia Story* (1940); the television productions, *The Glass Menagerie* (1973) and *The Corn Is Green* (1979); and the Broadway shows, *The Philadelphia Story* (1939), *As You Like It* (1950), *The Millionaires* (1952), *Coco* (1969), and *The West Side Waltz* (1981).

I was born on November 8, 1907, in Hartford, Connecticut. While attending Bryn Mawr, I became interested in acting. I went on to study acting with Frances Robinson-Duff and dancing with Mordkin. My first leading role was in *The Big Pond* (1930), in which I was fired my first night on the stage. In 1932, I was replaced by Ann Harding in *The Animal Kingdom* (1932). Then I made my Broadway debut in *Death Takes a Holiday* (1934); again I was fired. If I would have given up, I would not have realized my first success in *Art & Mrs. Bottle* (1931). My success continued on the stage in *The Warrior's Husband* (1932), which brought me several Hollywood offers. I made my film debut in *A Bill of Divorcement* (1932), which brought me instant stardom.

WHO AM I?

1. I was born on November 8, 1907, in Hartford, Connecticut.
2. I was labeled "box office poison" by Hollywood in 1938.
3. In 1934, I won my first Academy Award for *Morning Glory* (1933).
4. I played opposite Cary Grant in *Little Women* (1933), *Bringing Up Baby* (1938), *Holiday* (1938), and *The Philadelphia Story* (1940).
5. I partnered with Spencer Tracy in nine films; for one of those films, *Guess Who's Coming to Dinner* (1967), I won my second Academy Award in 1968.

My successful bit parts in *The Asphalt Jungle* (1950) and *All About Eve* (1950), led to my starring roles in *Gentlemen Prefer Blondes* (1953), *How to Marry a Millionaire* (1953), and *The Seven Year Itch* (1955). These films established me as a sex symbol and comedienne.

But I longed to receive recognition for my dramatic ability, so I left Hollywood to study with Lee Strasberg at the Actors Studio in New York. After my two year absence from Hollywood, I returned to star in more dramatic films, such as *Bus Stop* (1956), *The Prince and the Showgirl* (1957), *Some Like It Hot* (1959), and *The Misfits* (1961), my last film. On August 5, 1962, I died from an overdose of sleeping pills in my Hollywood, California, home.

I was born Norma Jean Mortenson on July 1, 1926, in Los Angeles, California. While a photographer's model my nude picture appeared on a calendar, which led to a one-year contract with 20th Century–Fox at a $125 a week and my film debut in *Scudda Hoo! Scudda Hay!* (1948). My scene was cut from the film before it was released and the studio decided not to renew my contract.

For my brief performances in *All About Eve* (1950), 20th Century–Fox signed me to a new seven-year contract with a $3,500 a week option. A string of minor roles followed, until I received starring roles in *Don't Bother to Knock, Full House, Clash by Night, We're Not Married, Niagara*, and *Monkey Business*, all filmed in 1952.

WHO AM I?

1. My third husband, playwright Arthur Miller, wrote the play *After the Fall* (1964) about our unhappy marriage.
2. My dramatic roles include *Bus Stop* (1956) and *The Misfits* (1961).
3. I starred in a handful of comedies: *Gentlemen Prefer Blondes* (1953), *How to Marry a Millionaire* (1953), *The Seven Year Itch* (1955), *The Prince and the Showgirl* (1957), and *Some Like It Hot* (1959).
4. On August 5, 1962, I died at the age of 36 of an overdose of sleeping pills.
5. I was born Norma Jean Mortenson (Baker) on June 1, 1926, in Los Angeles, California.

8 I am best remembered for my motion picture musicals from the 1930s through the 1950s. My talented dance partner Ginger Rogers and I starred in such musical hits as, *Flying Down to Rio* (1933), *Top Hat* (1935), *Roberta* (1935), and *Shall We Dance?* (1937). My finest moments include an Academy Award nomination for *The Towering Inferno* (1974) and nine Emmy Awards for my television variety show, *An Evening with . . .* (you know who?), which debuted in 1958.

My life began as Fred Austerlitz on May 10, 1899, in Omaha, Nebraska. At the age of four, I began taking ballet lessons with my sister Adele. Our parents noticed our special talent and enrolled us in a dancing, singing, and dramatic school in New York. Just two years later (1906), we were making appearances on the vaudeville stage. In 1917, we made our Broadway debut in *Over the Top*, which lead to a series of musical hits: *For Goodness Sake* (1922), *Lady Be Good* (1925), and *The Band Wagon* (1931).

WHO AM I?

1. I made my vaudeville debut in 1908, with my sister Adele.
2. I began my screen career with *Dancing Lady* (1933).
3. My Broadway shows include: *Over the Top* (1917), *Lady Be Good* (1925), and *The Band Wagon* (1931).
4. My films include: *Flying Down to Rio* (1933), *Roberta* (1935), *Top Hat* (1935), *Shall We Dance?* (1937), *Royal Wedding* (1951), *Daddy Long Legs* (1955), etc.
5. I was born Fred Austerlitz on May 10, 1899, in Omaha, Nebraska.

9 My motion picture role in *Broadway Melody* (1938), established me as a singing star and film celebrity. I went on to make several movies with my dear friend Mickey Rooney, including *Love Finds Andy Hardy* (1938), *Life Begins for Andy Hardy* (1941), and *Girl Crazy* (1943). In my 15 years with MGM, I appeared in about 35 films, including *The Wizard of Oz* (1938), which made me a star; *For Me and My Gal* (1941), my first adult role; *Meet Me in St. Louis* (1944); and *A Star* *is Born* (1954). I won a special Academy Award for the song, "Over the Rainbow" (performed in the film, *The Wizard of Oz*). My singing and dancing career blossomed at the Palace Theatre in New York, with a record-setting vaudeville performance of 19 weeks, 184 performances (1951–1952).

I was born Frances Gumm on June 10, 1922, in Grand Rapids, Minnesota. My first stage performance occurred when I was only two-and-a-half, singing "Jingle Bells" in a Christmas pageant. From that point on, I knew the stage was for me. With my sisters, I put together a song and dance trio, accompanied by our mother on the piano. Our first appearance was at the Biltmore Hotel in Los Angeles, then we went on a nation-wide tour. While singing the song, "Dinah" (my favorite) in Lake Tahoe, an MGM Studios' agent signed me to a seven-year contract. I made my film debut in a two-reel short called *Every Sunday Afternoon* (1935). At the age of 14, after appearing on the Chase & Sanborn radio show, I performed my first stage performance at Loew's State Theatre in New York.

WHO AM I?

1. I began my career at the age of four, singing with my sisters in my father's theater.
2. I was born Frances Gumm on June 10, 1922, in Grand Rapids, Minnesota.
3. In 1935, I joined MGM and gained popularity in the Andy Hardy film series.
4. My film credits include: *Babes in Arms* (1939), *Meet Me in St. Louis* (1944), and *A Star Is Born* (1954).
5. I won a special Academy Award for the song, "Over the Rainbow" (performed in the film, *The Wizard of Oz*, 1938).

10

My first starring role in a Hollywood movie came in *High Noon* (1952). In 1953, I received an Academy Award nomination as best supporting actress for my role in the film *Mogambo*. Then I caught the eye of Alfred Hitchcock who cast me in three of his movies: *Rear Window* (1954), which made me a star; *Dial M for Murder* (1954); and *To Catch a Thief* (1955). More successful films followed: *The*

Country Girl (1954), for which I won an Academy Award for best actress; *The Swan* (1956); and my final film, *High Society* (1956), 11 movies in all. On April 18, 1956, I gave up my Hollywood film career to marry my fairy tale prince, Prince Rainier of Monaco.

I was born on November 12, 1929, in Philadelphia, Pennsylvania. In grammar school, I played the Virgin Mary in the annual Christmas play. I began to take a serious interest in acting when I was around nine or ten. When I was 12 (already performing on a regular basis with my sister Peggy at the East Falls Old Academy Players), I made my amateur theatrical debut in *Don't Feed the Animals* (1941). Shortly after graduating from Stevens High School (1947), I entered the Academy of Dramatic Arts in New York to pursue my theatrical ambitions. To support myself, I worked as a photographer's model and actress in television commercials. Then I made my professional debut in a revival of my Uncle George's play, *The Torch Bearers* (1949). The summer of 1951 brought me recognition in the plays *The Man Who Came to Dinner*, *The Cocktail Party*, and *Ring Around the Moon*.

WHO AM I?

1. I was born on November 12, 1929, in Philadelphia, Pennsylvania.
2. I made my professional debut in a revival of my Uncle George's play, *The Torch Bearers* (1949).
3. My first starring role in a Hollywood movie came in *High Noon* (1952).
4. I caught the eye of Alfred Hitchcock who cast me in three of his movies: *Rear Window* (1954), *Dial M for Murder* (1954), and *To Catch a Thief* (1955).
5. On April 18, 1956, I gave up my Hollywood film career to marry my fairy tale prince, Prince Rainier of Monaco.

After making some major changes in my life: bleaching my hair blonde, taking singing and acting lessons, and changing my name to my mother's maiden name (added a "y'), my film career began to take off. The B-movie, *Only Angels Have Wings* (1939), elevated me to new stardom. I went on to make the films *The Strawberry Blonde* (1941), *Blood and Sand* (1941), *You'll Never Get Rich* (1941; it made

me a star), *My Gal Sal* (1942), and *You Were Never Lovelier* (1942). By now, I was making $6,500 a week and was a leading actress in Hollywood. I went on to make several more films, including *The Cover Girl* (1944), *Gilda* (1946), *The Loves of Carmen* (1948), *Miss Sadie Thompson* (1953), and *Pal Joey* (1957).

I was born Margarita Carmen Cansino on October 17, 1918, in New York City, New York. When I was just 11, I made my stage debut in a school production. Later, I took dancing and acting lessons at Carthay School and Hamilton High School. My father (a wonderful dancer in his own right) saw that I had talent, so he took me on the road as his new dance partner. We had an 18-month run in Tijuana, Mexico, and a seven-month run at a resort in Aqua Caliente, Mexico. It was at the latter that I met a Fox Film Corp. executive, who hired me to play a supporting role in *Dante's Inferno* (1935) and signed me to a one-year contract. By the time I was 23, I had already made 32 films; 14 of these were B- or low-budget films made for Columbia.

WHO AM I?

1. I was born on October 17, 1918, in New York City, New York.
2. I bleached my hair blonde, took singing and acting lessons, and changed my name to my mother's maiden name (added a "y"), to get my film career off the ground.
3. A Fox Film Corp. executive hired me to play a supporting role in *Dante's Inferno* (1935).
4. I gained movie stardom with the films *The Strawberry Blonde* (1941), *My Gal Sal* (1942), and *You Were Never Lovelier* (1942).
5. I went on to make several more films, including *Gilda* (1946), *Miss Sadie Thompson* (1953), and *Pal Joey* (1957).

12 My film successes in *Captains Courageous* (1937) and *Boys Town* (1938) earned me two Academy Awards for best actor. I was also nominated for best actor in the films *Father of the Bride* (1950), *Bad Day at Black Rock* (1955), *The Old Man and the Sea* (1958), *Inherit the Wind* (1960), and *Judgment at Nuremburg* (1961). During my film career, I costarred with my dear friend Katharine Hepburn in nine films, including my last film, *Guess Who's Coming to Dinner?* (1968), which was released after my death. I starred in several other films, including *The Power and the Glory* (1933), *San Francisco* (1936), *Test Pilot* (1938), and *Boom Town* (1940).

I was born on April 5, 1900, in Milwaukee, Wisconsin. After being discharged from the Navy (World War I), I enrolled at Ripon College (1921). Here I was bitten by the acting bug when I was given a part in the campus production, *The Truth*. Soon after, I left Ripon to attend the American Academy of Dramatic Arts in New York, where I roomed with Pat O'Brien. My first job on Broadway was a $10 a week (later $15) non-speaking role as a robot in *Karel Capek's R.U.R.* (1922). Then I landed a part in a big New York production, *A Royal Fandango* (1923), which closed a short time later. Soon my luck changed when I starred in the stage production *The Last Mile* (1930), which allowed me to go to Hollywood and make my film debut in *Up the River* (1930). My career before the camera ended on June 10, 1967, in Beverly Hills, California.

WHO AM I?

1. I was born on April 5, 1900, in Milwaukee, Wisconsin.
2. As a top screen star for 40 years, I was known for my dramatic, sensitive character portrayals.
3. My last movie was *Guess Who's Coming to Dinner* (1968).
4. My film successes in *Captains Courageous* (1937) and *Boys Town* (1938) earned me two Academy Awards for best actor.
5. During my film career, I costarred with my dear friend Katharine Hepburn in nine films, including *Woman of the Year* (1942) and *Adam's Rib* (1949).

Chapter Five
Sports Figures

1

During my 22 seasons in major league baseball, I hit a record-setting 714 home runs (later broken by Hank Aaron). My peak came in 1927, when I hit 60; four different years I hit more than 50. In the ten World Series in which I played, I hit 15 home runs and was on the winning team seven times. My lifetime batting average was .342, and in my career I either set or tied 76 different batting or pitching records. I played in eight All-Star games (1926–1931, 1933, 1934) and was voted the MVP for the American League in 1923. For my prowess with the bat, I was nicknamed "the Sultan of Swat" and "the King of Clout." In 1936, I was chosen as one of the first players to be inducted into the Baseball Hall of Fame. I died on August 16, 1948, in New York City, New York.

I was born on February 6, 1895, in Baltimore, Maryland. It was under Brother Gilbert's direction at St. Mary's Industrial High School (Baltimore) that I learned to play the game of baseball. He was also instrumental in getting me my first professional baseball contract. At the age of 18 (1914), I was offered a $600 contract (for a six-month season) to play with the Baltimore team in the International League. My first professional game as a pitcher was against Connie Mack's Philadelphia Athletics in an exhibition game. During my first season, I played in 46 games with a batting average of .231 and a fielding average of .964; of those 46 games I pitched 35 with a record of 22 wins, 9 losses, and 4 ties. Before my first season ended, I was sold to the Boston Red Sox of the American League. Here I became an outstanding left-handed pitcher and a powerful hitter; the latter allowed me to play first base and outfield when I was not pitching. After hitting 29 home runs in 1919, the New York Yankees bought my contract (January 3, 1920) for $125,000.

WHO AM I?

1. I was born on February 6, 1895, in Baltimore, Maryland.
2. I was a pitcher until I moved to the outfield.
3. My real name is George Herman.
4. For my prowess with the bat, I was nicknamed "the Sultan of Swat" and "the King of Clout."
5. During my 22 seasons (1914–1935) in major league baseball, I hit a record-setting 714 home runs (later broken by Hank Aaron).

2 In 1957 (at the age of 30), I won the Women's Singles Championship at Wimbledon. That same year, I won the Women's National Singles Championship at the U.S. Open, along with the French, Italian, and Asian titles, making me the top women's tennis player in the world. The following year, I won both the U.S. Open and Wimbledon titles. Earlier in my career (1950), I broke the color barrier in tennis by playing in the U.S. Open (Forest Hills, New York). I lost in the second round, but my playing made a great contribution to my growing career and the future of the sport. I retired in 1959 (at the age of 32), trading in my tennis racket for golf clubs. Four years later, I broke the color barrier in professional golf with my astounding drives of 260 yards.

I was born on August 25, 1927, in Silver, South Carolina. At the age of 13, my father taught me how to box, but it was my skill with a paddle tennis racket that caught Buddy Walker's (summer playground leader) eye. He convinced me to try tennis, and I started by hitting balls up against a wall at a nearby park. My skills progressed rapidly with the help of the Cosmopolitan Club members, who paid for my tennis lessons with Fred Johnson and for a junior membership to the club. Almost a year later, I entered the American Tennis Association's New York State Open Championship (a mostly black tournament) in the girl's single division and won. At the Williston Industrial High School, I was captain and star of the girl's basketball team and even practiced with the boy's basketball and baseball teams, all the while going to daily tennis practices. Then I won an athletic scholarship to Florida A & M. After a fulfilling professional career in tennis and golf, I became the Recreation Supervisor for the Essex County Parks Commission.

WHO AM I?

1. I was born on August 25, 1927, in Silver, South Carolina.
2. While at the Williston Industrial High School, I was captain and star of the girl's basketball team.
3. At the age of 13, my skill with a paddle tennis racket caught Buddy Walker's eye.
4. In 1950, I broke the color barrier in tennis by playing in the U.S. Open (Forest Hills, New York).
5. In 1957 (at the age of 30), I won the Women's Singles Championship at Wimbledon. That same year, I won the Women's National Singles Championship at the U.S. Open, along with the French, Italian, and Asian titles.

3

From 1937 to 1949, I held the title of world heavyweight champion (defended my title 11 times). To win the title (June 22, 1937), I knocked out James J. Braddock to become the youngest boxer ever to win the title. After I won my first eight professional bouts, I was nicknamed the "Brown Bomber." I gained national recognition when I knocked out Stanley Poreda and Lee Ramagl, which led to my 1935 fight with Max Baer, who I defeated in four rounds. The following year, I was knocked out by Max Schmeling in 12 rounds, but I got my revenge in our second bout when I knocked him out in the first round. My boxing career consisted of 68 wins (54 knockouts, 13 decisions, and 1 disqualification) with only 3 losses. In 1949, I retired as an undefeated champion and was inducted into the Boxing Hall of Fame in 1954. I died on April 12, 1981.

I was born on May 13, 1914, in Lexington (near Lafayette), Alabama. As an ice-wagon driver, I developed strong shoulder muscles, which would come in handy years later. At the age of 16, I became a sparring partner in a Detroit gymnasium. In my first local fight, I was knocked down six times in three rounds. I could have given up, but instead I went on to win my next three bouts. To support my family, I went to work at the Ford auto plant (Detroit), while boxing as an amateur. In 1934, I won the National A.A.U. light-heavyweight title. With renewed confidence, I turned professional three months later and dropped my last name (used my first and middle name).

WHO AM I?

1. My boxing career consisted of 68 wins (54 knockouts, 13 decisions, and 1 disqualification) with only 3 losses.
2. In 1949, I retired as an undefeated champion and was inducted into the Boxing Hall of Fame in 1954.
3. By order of President Ronald Reagan, I was buried in Arlington National Cemetery on April 12, 1981.
4. I was born Joseph L. Barrow on May 13, 1914, in Lexington (near Lafayette), Alabama.
5. After I won my first eight professional bouts, I was nicknamed the "Brown Bomber."

My trademark of charging to victory in the late rounds of a tournament endeared me to my fans, who were nicknamed "Arnie's Army." In the six years after turning professional, I took first place in more than 20 tournaments. I won the Masters in 1958,

1960, 1962, and 1964, making me the first golfer in the history of the game to win the title four times. By 1967, I had become the first professional golfer to reach the $1 million mark. For my successes on the links, I was named Golfer of the Year (1960 and 1962) and the Golfer of the Decade (1960s). My love of golf continues today, with my appearances in Senior tournaments and Skins Games, with fellow senior greats.

I was born on September 10, 1929, in Youngstown, Pennsylvania. When I was just three years old, I got my first golf club. At the age of nine, I shot an amazing 45 for nine holes. While on the Latrobe High School golf team (four years), I won the Western Pennsylvania Junior three times and the Western Pennsylvania Amateur five times, while only losing one match. In 1947, I received a golf scholarship to Wake Forest University, where I majored in business administration. I won several amateur tournaments, including the United States Amateur (1954). That same year, I turned professional and won my first professional tournament: the Canadian Open in August 1955.

WHO AM I?

1. I was born on September 10, 1929, in Youngstown, Pennsylvania.
2. While on the Latrobe High School golf team I won the Western Pennsylvania Junior three times and the Western Pennsylvania Amateur five times, while only losing one match.
3. By 1967, I had become the first professional golfer to reach the $1 million mark.
4. I won the Masters in 1958, 1960, 1962, and 1964, making me the first golfer in the history of the game to win the title four times.
5. My trademark of charging to victory in the late rounds of a tournament endeared me to my fans, who were nicknamed "Arnie's Army."

5 At the 1932 Los Angeles Olympics, I broke two women's world records, in the javelin throw (143 feet, 4 inches) and the 80-meter hurdles (11.7 seconds). That same year, I won the National Women's Track and Field Championship by earning 30 individual points against a 22 member Illinois team that finished second. In 1934, I turned to golf, winning the Texas Women's Golf Association Championship

(1935), the Women's Eastern Open Championship (1935), and the Women's Western Open Championship (1940). I won my first 18 tournaments before I suffered a loss, an impressive feat in any sport. After conquering golf I turned to tennis and was coached by Eleanor Tennant. For my exploits, the press dubbed me "Muscle Moll."

I was born on June 26, 1914, in Port Arthur, Texas. Growing up, I excelled in all the sports: hitting home runs for the boy's baseball team, playing ball for the Beaumont Senior High School girl's basketball team, receiving 92 track and field medals, and setting records in lifesaving, figure skating, and diving. At the age of 16, I was asked to play on the Golden Cyclone Athletic Club's basketball team (made up of the best girl basketball players in the country). In my two years with the team, I was chosen an All-American forward both years. I also owned the Southern A.A.U. track and field records in all the events that I entered. Stricken with cancer, I died on September 27, 1956, in Galveston, Texas.

WHO AM I?

1. I was born on June 26, 1914, in Port Arthur, Texas.
2. At the age of 16, I was asked to play on the Golden Cyclone Athletic Club's basketball team.
3. In 1934, I turned to golf, winning the Texas Women's Golf Association Championship (1935), the Women's Eastern Open Championship (1935), and the Women's Western Open Championship (1940).
4. In the 1932 Los Angeles Olympics, I broke two women's world records, in the javelin throw (143 feet, 4 inches) and the 80-meter hurdles (11.7 seconds).
5. For my exploits, the press dubbed me "Muscle Moll." I was also nicknamed "The Texas Babe."

My "rope-a-dope" style led to three separate world heavyweight titles. The first title came on February 25, 1964, when I beat Sonny Liston in the sixth round. In 1967, my title was taken away after I refused to be drafted, claiming exemption as a Black Muslim minister. I reclaimed the title from George Foreman on October 30, 1974. Four years later (1978), I lost the title to Leon Spinks, but I reclaimed it later that same year. Before turning professional in October 1960, I won the Amateur Athletic Union's light heavyweight title, the National Golden Gloves heavyweight title, and topped it off by winning an Olympic Gold medal.

I was born Cassius Marcellus Clay, Jr., on January 17, 1942, in Louisville, Kentucky. My boxing career began at the age of 12 after reporting my bicycle had been stolen to Joe Elsby Martin, a police officer who ran the boxing program in the basement of the Columbia Auditorium. Under his supervision I trained two hours a day, then I went off to train with Fred Stoner (taught me everything about boxing) at the Grace Community Center for four hours. I went on to win 100 out of 108 bouts as an amateur, capturing six Kentucky Golden Glove titles. After turning professional I won 19 bouts (15 by knockout), before winning the world heavyweight title.

WHO AM I?

1. Before turning professional in October 1960, I won the Amateur Athletic Union's light heavyweight title, the National Golden Gloves heavyweight title, and topped it off by winning an Olympic Gold medal.
2. In 1967, my title was taken away after I refused to be drafted, claiming exemption as a Black Muslim minister.
3. I beat Sonny Liston on February 25, 1964, to win the world heavyweight title.
4. My "rope-a-dope" style led to three separate world heavyweight titles.
5. I was born Cassius Marcellus Clay, Jr., on January 17, 1942, in Louisville, Kentucky.

7

I became one of baseball's greatest outfielders with my defensive plays in center field and my powerful right-handed hitting at the plate. During my years with the New York Yankees (1935–1951; missed the 1943, 1944, and 1945 seasons because of World War II), I set a major league record by hitting safely in 56 consecutive games (May 15 to July 16, 1941). I captured the American League batting championships in 1939 (.381 average) and 1940 (.352 average); and was voted the league's MVP in 1939, 1941, and 1947. The New York fans nicknamed me the "Yankee Clipper" and the "Big Guy." I compiled a lifetime batting average of .325, with 361 home runs in 1,736 games. During my career, I also played in 10 World Series and 11 All-Star games. For my efforts, I was inducted into the Baseball Hall of Fame in 1955.

My life began on November 25, 1914, in Martinez, California. At the age of 14, I received an $8 merchandise order for playing baseball in the Boys Club League and helping my team win the championship that year. By the time I was 17, I was playing ball with the minor league club, the San Francisco Seals (my older brother Vince was also a member of the team) of the Pacific Coast League. I started out at shortstop, but was moved to the outfield because of my strong arm. The next year, I batted .340 and broke a league record by hitting safely in 61 straight games. By 1934, the New Yankees had bought my contract from the Seals, but decided I should stay with them one more year to gain experience. I batted .398 with 34 home runs, and was voted MVP for 1935. The following season, I moved up to the Yankees and batted .323 with a fielding percentage of .978.

WHO AM I?

1. My life began on November 25, 1914, in Martinez, California.
2. My baseball career began with the San Francisco Seals of the Pacific Coast League.
3. I played in 10 World Series and 11 All-Star games. In 1955, I was inducted into the Baseball Hall of Fame.
4. During my years with the New York Yankees (1936–1951), I set a major league record by hitting safely in 56 consecutive games (May 15 to July 16, 1941).
5. The New York fans nicknamed me the "Yankee Clipper" and the "Big Guy."

8   I became the first NBA player in the history of the game to reach the 3,000 point plateau. On March 2, 1962, I scored an astounding 100 points in a high scoring game (169–147) against the New York Knickerbockers. Earlier, at the University of Kansas (in my first varsity game), I scored a record 52 points against Northwestern University. In 1960, I obtained another first by winning both the league's

Rookie of the Year and MVP awards. I went on to lead the NBA in scoring (39.6 points per game) for the next seven years. I left the game with a career average of over 30 points per game, and for 11 seasons I led the NBA in rebounding. I was nicknamed "Wilt the Stilt."

My life began on August 21, 1936, in Philadelphia, Pennsylvania. I began to concentrate on basketball as a teenager at Shoemaker Junior High School. By the time I entered Overbrook High School (1952), basketball was all I thought about. In the next three years, I scored 2,252 points, which caught the attention of 77 major universities and 125 smaller colleges. I turned down all the other offers in order to play at the University of Kansas. During my two years on the varsity squad, I averaged 30 points per game, was named to the All-American team both years, and our team won 42 out of 50 games. I left the University of Kansas after my junior year to play one year with the Harlem Globetrotters.

WHO AM I?

1. My life began on August 21, 1936, in Philadelphia, Pennsylvania.
2. I played a year with the Harlem Globetrotters before signing with the Philadelphia Warriors in 1958.
3. In my first varsity game at the University of Kansas, I scored 52 points against Northwestern University.
4. On March 2, 1962, I scored an astounding 100 points in a high scoring game (169–147) against the New York Knickerbockers.
5. I was nicknamed "Wilt the Stilt."

9

Considered to be the fastest fighter in the ring, I held the welterweight title from 1946 to 1951 and the middleweight title on five separate occasions between 1951 and 1960. In my first six years as a professional, I won 73 bouts and only lost 1 (to Jake La Motta). In 1951, I had to give up my welterweight title when I knocked out Jake La Motta for the middleweight title (in those days you could not hold both). I ended my boxing career in 1965, after 25 years in the ring. During those years, I compiled a career record of 175 wins (109 by knockouts) and 27 losses (18 lost by decisions). I was inducted into the Boxing Hall of Fame in 1967.

I was born Walker Smith on May 3, 1920, in Detroit, Michigan. When I was 12, I joined the amateur boxing ranks in New York City (my family moved there from Detroit). Then I quit school so I could train at the Salem Crescent gymnasium with George Gainford, who remained my trainer and manager throughout my professional boxing career. Under his direction, I went on to win all my amateur bouts, including the 1939 Golden Glove featherweight championship and 1939 Golden Glove lightweight championship. Being under the age requirement to box, I took the name of another amateur boxer and added a little bit of "sugar." Then I turned professional as a lightweight in 1940.

WHO AM I?

1. I was born Walker Smith on May 3, 1920, in Detroit, Michigan.
2. In my first six years as a professional, I won 73 bouts and only lost 1 (to Jake La Motta).
3. During my 25 years in the ring, I compiled a career record of 175 wins (109 by knockouts) and 27 losses (18 lost by decisions).
4. I held the welterweight title from 1946 to 1951 and the middleweight title on five separate occasions between 1951 and 1960.
5. Being under the age requirement to box, I took the name of another amateur boxer and added a little bit of "sugar."

10

I broke onto the tennis scene in 1962 (at the age of 18) by upsetting Margaret Smith (Court), the world's number one-ranked women's tennis player, in the first round at Wimbledon. In 1967, I became the first woman since 1951 to win three Wimbledon titles in one year. That same phenomenal year, I won the United States Open at Forest Hills, New York. I went on to win a record 20 Wimbledon titles, which includes six women's singles titles (1966, 1967, 1968, 1972, 1973, and 1975); ten women's double titles (1961, 1962, 1965, 1967, 1968, 1970, 1971, 1972, 1973, and 1979); and four mixed doubles titles (1967, 1971, 1973, and 1974). My other accomplishments include: four United States Open women's singles titles (1967, 1971, 1972, and 1974), the Australian Open women's singles title (1968), and the French Open women's singles title (1972). I will forever be remembered for my much publicized tennis match ("Battle of the Sexes") in 1973 against Bobby Riggs, a 55 year old former men's champion.

My life began on November 22, 1943, in Long Beach, California. After finding the girl's softball team limiting, my parents suggested that I play tennis. At the age of 11, my father got me involved in the city's tennis program. That same year, I played my first tennis match against a college junior and won. My love for tennis grew, and throughout high school I played after school and on weekends, and during the summer months I played every day to improve my game. At the age of 15, Alice Marble (a great tennis star in her own right) began giving me lessons. Through her efforts, my national ranking quickly moved from 19th to 4th. That same year (1958), I won my first tennis title in the Southern California Junior Championship. Despite injuries and operations later in my career, I dominated women's tennis with my serve-and-volley play.

WHO AM I?

1. I was born on November 22, 1943, in Long Beach, California.
2. At the age of 15, Alice Marble began giving me lessons, and my national ranking quickly moved from 19th to 4th.
3. I broke onto the tennis scene in 1962 by upsetting Margaret Smith (Court) in the first round at Wimbledon.
4. In 1967, I became the first woman since 1951 to win three Wimbledon titles in one year.
5. I will forever be remembered for my much publicized tennis match ("Battle of the Sexes") in 1973 against Bobby Riggs, a 55 year old former men's champion.

The highlight of my career came in 1974 when I broke Babe Ruth's lifetime home run record of 714. On April 4th of that year, I tied the record in Cincinnati. Four days later (on April 8th) in Atlanta, I hit number 715 off Al Downing of the Los Angeles Dodgers. I broke into the major leagues with the Milwaukee Braves (Braves later moved to Atlanta in 1966) in 1954, and became their starting right fielder. For my powerful hitting and exceptional fielding, I earned the National League's batting championship two times (1956 and 1959); the MVP award (1957); led the league in home runs four times (1957, 1963, 1966, and 1967); runs batted in four times (1957, 1960, 1963, and 1966); and received the Golden Glove Award three times (1958, 1959, and 1960). I retired at the conclusion of the 1976 season, with a career batting average of .305, 3,771 hits, 2,297 runs batted in, and 755 home runs. I was inducted into the Baseball Hall of Fame in 1982.

I was born on February 5, 1934, in Mobile, Alabama. As a child, I played sand-lot baseball for the Pritchett Athletics. In 1952, the Mobile Black Bears (a local team in the Negro League) asked me to play in an exhibition game against the Indianapolis Clowns. The Clowns were so impressed by my play that they signed me to a $200 a month contract. The owner of the Clowns, Syd Pollock saw my potential and wrote a letter to the Milwaukee Braves, who bought my contract for $10,000 (June 12, 1952). I spent my first year with the Braves' Class C Northern League team in Eau Claire, Wisconsin, as an infielder (shortstop). After batting .336 and being named Rookie of the Year, I played the 1953 season with the Braves' Class A South Atlantic (Sally) League team in Jacksonville, Florida, where I was moved to second base. Here I led the league in batting, runs batted in, doubles, runs scored, and total bases.

WHO AM I?

1. I was born on February 5, 1934, in Mobile, Alabama.
2. My professional baseball career began in the infield with the Braves' Class C Northern League team in 1952.
3. In 1954, I broke into the major leagues with the Milwaukee Braves and became their starting right fielder.
4. I retired with 755 home runs and was inducted into the Baseball Hall of Fame in 1982.
5. The highlight of my career came in 1974 when I broke Babe Ruth's lifetime home run record of 714.

12 My professional football career began in 1957 when the Cleveland Browns chose me as their first round draft pick. During my nine years with the Browns, I led the NFL in rushing eight times; I gained a total 12,312 yards rushing (5.2 yards per carry) and held 10 of the 17 NFL rushing records. I started every game (118 games), and I scored 126 touchdowns (5 touchdowns in one game, 1959). My best season ever was 1963, when I gained 1,863 yards rushing (6.4 yards per carry) to set an NFL rushing record. For my outstanding play, I was chosen the NFL's Player of the Year for 1963 (also in 1958). After nine brilliant, but grueling years in the NFL, I retired in 1966 to pursue a career in acting. In 1971, I was inducted into the Professional Football Hall of Fame.

I was born on February 17, 1936, on St. Simons Island, Georgia. At the age of 14, I played on the Manhasset High School first-string football team. There (besides football) I excelled in lacrosse, basketball, and baseball, and was named one of New York's best athletes. My senior year, I received 42 college scholarship offers and gained the attention of the New York Yankees and the Boston Braves. After graduation I went onto Syracuse University, where I earned ten varsity letters; three in football, three in lacrosse, two in basketball, and two in track. In 1956, both the Associated Press and the United Press International chose me an All-American (Syracuse's first All-American half-back); I also earned All-American honors in lacrosse.

WHO AM I?

1. I was born on February 17, 1936, in St. Simons Island, Georgia.
2. I was an All-American in lacrosse at Syracuse University.
3. My professional football career began in 1957, when the Cleveland Browns chose me as their first round draft pick.
4. My best season ever was 1963, when I gained 1,863 yards rushing to set an NFL rushing record.
5. During my nine years with the Cleveland Browns, I led the NFL in rushing eight times, gained a total 12,312 yards rushing, and scored 126 touchdowns.

Chapter Six
Writers

1

My most successful work, *The Scarlet Letter* (1850), has since become recognized as a literary masterpiece. It also established me as one of the best fiction writers of the 19th century. I also gained success with *The House of Seven Gables* (1851), which is now considered a classic. *A Wonder Book for Girls and Boys* (1852) and *Tanglewood Tales* (1853) were both very popular children's books. My other children's books include: *Grandfather's Chair* (1841), *Liberty Tree* (1841), and *Biographical Stories for Children* (1842). My later works include: *The Life of Franklin Pierce* (1852), *Marble Faun* (1860), and *Our Old Home* (1863). I died in my sleep on May 19, 1864, in Plymouth, New Hampshire, with four uncompleted novels that were later published.

I was born on July 4, 1804, in Salem, Massachusetts. Due to a foot injury and health problems as a child, my interest in books flourished. While working for my family's stagecoach business, I developed an interest in writing. Through the encouragement of my mother's family, I attended Bowdoin College to further my writing skills. Here I published the novel *Fanshawe* (1828), which I published with my own money. Early works, such as *Provincial Tales* (1829), *The Story Teller* (failed to be published), and *Mr. Higginbotham's Catastrophe* (1834), brought me little success. It was not until I used my own name (previous works were anonymous) that my writing became successful (*Twice-Told Tales*, 1937).

WHO AM I?

1. I was born on July 4, 1804, in Salem, Massachusetts.
2. While attending Bowdoin College, I published the novel *Fanshawe* (1928) with my own money.

3. My children's books include: *Grandfather's Chair* (1841), *Liberty Tree* (1841), and *Tanglewood Tales* (1853).
4. I gained success with the novel, *The House of Seven Gables* (1851), which is now considered a classic.
5. My most successful work, *The Scarlet Letter* (1850), has since become recognized as a literary masterpiece.

2

My trademark of lean, brutal subjects was first seen in a collection of short stories called *In Our Time* (1925). The following year, my first major novel, *The Sun Also Rises* (1926), brought me instant fame that lasted until my death on July 2, 1961, in Ketchum, Idaho, of a self-inflicted gunshot wound. I produced five more novels: *A Farewell to Arms* (1929), *To Have and Have Not* (1937), *For Whom the Bell Tolls* (1940), *Across the River and Into the Trees* (1950), and *The Old Man and the Sea* (1952), my last published work. Also, I wrote more than 50 short stories, some of which were collected in three major books: *In Our Time* (1925), *Men Without Women* (1927), and *Winner Take Nothing* (1933). I am also widely known for such tales as "The Killers" (1927), "The Snows of Kilimanjaro" (1938), and "The Short Happy Life of Francis Macomber" (1938).

I was born on July 21, 1899, in Oak Park, Illinois. My interest in writing blossomed in high school, where I wrote columns for my school's newspaper. After graduation, I headed to Missouri to work for the Kansas City *Star*. Here I learned the fundamentals of writing, which proved beneficial to my future writing career. During World War I, I worked as an ambulance driver for the Red Cross and as a foreign correspondent for the *Toronto Star*. These experiences provided me with material for future novels. My other works include: my only play, *The Fifth Column* (1938), and my non-fiction volumes, *Death in the Afternoon* (1932), *Green Hills of Africa* (1935), and *A Moveable Feast* (1964).

WHO AM I?

1. I was born on July 21, 1899, in Oak Park, Illinois.
2. After graduation from high school, I headed to Missouri to work as a reporter for the Kansas City *Star*.

3. I won the 1953 Pulitzer Prize and the 1954 Nobel Prize for Literature.
4. I died on July 2, 1961, in Ketchum, Idaho, of a self-inflicted gunshot wound.
5. I am best-known for *The Old Man and the Sea* (1952), *For Whom the Bell Tolls* (1940), *The Sun Also Rises* (1926), and *A Farewell to Arms* (1929).

3 Fame first came to me with the novel *Of Mice and Men* (1937), which was also an award-winning play. My career reached new heights with the publication of my next novel, *The Grapes of Wrath* (1939), which was on the best sellers' list for two straight years. It also won a Pulitzer Prize for fiction and a National Book Award. To escape my new found celebrity status, I fled to Mexico (1940) to make a film documentary called *Forgotten Village* (became a non-fiction book in 1941). I gained renewed success with the novel *Cannery Row* (1945) and my third play-novelette, *East of Eden* (1952). My later works include: *The Winter of Discontent* (1961), which led to my Nobel Prize in literature in 1962; *Travels with Charley* (1962); and *America and Americans* (1966). I died on December 20, 1968, in New York City, New York.

I was born on February 27, 1902, in Salinas, California. After graduating from Sanford University I worked at various odd jobs, before getting my first novel, *Cup of Gold* (1929), published at the age of 27. *Cup of Gold* was not very successful, so I briefly turned to playwriting. The play *Pastures of Heaven* (1932), however, was much more successful and is considered one of my best works. The following year, my second novel, *To a God Unknown* (1933), met with the same fate as my first novel. Later, my luck changed with my third novel, *Tortilla Flat* (1935). My fourth novel, *In Dubious Battle* (1936), won critical acclaim, as did my next novel, *Their Blood Is Strong* (1938), a collection of newspaper articles; both were written while living among migrant farm workers.

WHO AM I?

1. I was born on February 27, 1902, in Salinas, California.
2. My first novel, *Cup of Gold* (1929), was not very successful, so I briefly turned to playwriting.

3. My later works include: *The Winter of Discontent* (1961), *Travels with Charley* (1962), and *America and Americans* (1966).
4. My career reached new heights with the publication of my novel *The Grapes of Wrath* (1939).
5. I am best remembered for my works *Of Mice and Men* (1937), *Cannery Row* (1945), and *East of Eden* (1952).

 My biggest success, *The Great Gatsby* (1925), brought me recognition for my contribution to the jazz era. After the poor reception of my longest novel, *Tender Is the Night* (1934), I moved to Hollywood to pursue a career in scriptwriting (sold two stories to the movies). Basing my fiction on my real-life experiences, I wrote many short stories which I collected into several volumes. These volumes include: *Flappers and Philosophers* (1921), *Tales of the Jazz Age* (1922), *All the Sad Young Men* (1926), *Taps at Reveille* (1935), and *The Crack Up* (1945). I also had some minor success with my novel *The Beautiful and Damned* (1922). My half-completed novel *The Last Tycoon* (1941) was published after my death on December 21, 1940, of a heart attack.

I was born Francis Scott Key on September 24, 1896, in St. Paul, Minnesota. At Princeton, I wrote shows for the Triangle Club, while my studies faltered. Instead of trying to improve my grades, I spent all my free time drafting a novel called *The Romantic Egoist*. Charles Scribner's and Sons rejected the finished manuscript, so I went to work at a New York advertising agency and made plans to marry my fair Zelda. We soon broke off the engagement, however, and I returned to St. Paul to work on my novel again. This time Charles Scribner's accepted it under the new name *This Side of Paradise* (1920), which brought me instant success. This success allowed me to find magazine markets for almost all of my short stories and enough money to marry Zelda at last.

WHO AM I?

1. I was born on September 24, 1896, in St. Paul, Minnesota.
2. At Princeton, I wrote shows for the Triangle Club.
3. My last two collections of short stories were *All the Sad Young Men* (1926) and *Taps at Reveille* (1935).

4. Charles Scribner's and Sons rejected my first novel *The Romantic Egoist*, which they later published under the new name *This Side of Paradise* (1920).
5. My most famous works include: *The Great Gatsby* (1925), *Tender Is the Night* (1934), and *The Last Tycoon* (1941).

During my lifetime, I gained little recognition from my writing. My novel *Moby-Dick* (1851) is now regarded as a 19th century classic. My love of the sea and the experiences I found on my voyages produced the material for which all my books and poetry have been based. I gained some fame with my novel *Billy Budd* (1924). My other books include: *Omoo* (1847), *Mardi and a Voyage Thithed* (1849), *White Jacket* (1850), *Pierre* (1855), *Israel Potter* (1855), and *The Confidence Man* (1857). After *The Confidence Man*, I gave up my pursuit of a writing career to devote myself to writing poetry, which I did for my own pleasure. My poetry includes a collection of Civil War poems called *Battle Pieces* (1866) and *Clarel: A Poem and Pilgrimage in the Holy Land* (1876).

My life began on August 1, 1819, in New York City, New York. Instead of attending college, I became a clerk at my uncle's bank and later taught school. Seeking a better way of life, I signed on with a ship headed for Liverpool, England. But instead of riches, I gained experiences that I would later write about with the encouragement of my family. From this first experience at sea, I wrote the novel *Reburn: His First Voyage* (1849). My first novel, *Typee: A Peep at Polynesian Life* (1846), was written about a later whaling voyage. After a disappointing writing career, I died virtually unknown on September 28, 1891, in New York City, New York.

WHO AM I?

1. I was born on August 1, 1819, in New York City, New York.
2. From my first experience at sea (Liverpool, England), I wrote the novel *Reburn: His First Voyage* (1949).
3. My other books include: *White Jacket* (1850), *Israel Potter* (1855), and *The Confidence Man* (1857).
4. *Billy Budd* (1924) recaptured my earliest adventures and enjoyed enormous success.
5. My novel *Moby-Dick* (1851) is now regarded as a 19th century classic.

6   *Uncle Tom's Cabin* (1852) brought me enormous success and has since become an all-time American classic. It was originally called *Life Among the Lowly* and appeared as a series in an antislavery paper, the *National Era* (Washington, DC). Within just a year, the book sold 300,000 copies. Because of its strong opinions, it has been considered one of the major reasons for the start of the Civil War. A year later, I wrote the sequel, *A Key to Uncle Tom's Cabin* (1853). My second antislavery novel, *Dred: A Tale of the Great Dismal Swamp* (1856), did not fair as well as the first, so I turned my attentions to writing about Puritan life in New England. These books include: *The Minister's Wooing* (1859), *The Pearl of Orr's Island* (1862), and *Oldtown Folks* (1870). I also wrote several children's books, including *Queer Little People* (1867), *Little Pussy Willow* (1870), and *Betty's Bright Idea* (1876).

I was born on June 14, 1811, in Litchfield, Connecticut. After attending the Litchfield Academy, I became a student-teacher at the Hartford Female

Seminary, where I was later put on staff in 1829. Three years later, I moved to Cincinnati, Ohio, where I continued teaching until 1850. Near exhaustion from overwork, I turned to writing. My first attempts at writing were published in the *Western Monthly Magazine*, the *New York Evangelist*, and several other magazines. My collaboration with my sister resulted in the *First Geography for Children* (1833), which brought us much success. Then I decided to go it alone with my first book, *The Mayflower: Sketches and Scenes and Characters Among the Descendents of the Puritans* (1843). I died on July 1, 1896, in Hartford, Connecticut.

WHO AM I?

1. I was born on June 14, 1811, in Litchfield, Connecticut.
2. My second antislavery novel, *Dred: A Tale of the Great Dismal Swamp* (1856), did not fair as well as my first.
3. My books on Puritan life include: *The Minister's Wooing* (1859), *The Pearl of Orr's Island* (1862), and *Oldtown Folks* (1870).
4. My children's books include *Queer Little People* (1867), *Little Pussy Willow* (1870), and *Betty's Bright Idea* (1876).
5. *Uncle Tom's Cabin* (1852) brought me enormous success.

7

I am considered one of the greatest humorists and writers of the 19th century. My two novels *The Adventures of Tom Sawyer* (1876) and *The Adventures of Huckleberry Finn* (1884) were my most successful works. Earlier I had gained fame with my humorous piece "The Celebrated Jumping Frog of Calaveras County" (1865). My fortunes continued with *The Innocents Abroad* (1869). Other works include: *The Gilded Age* (1873), *The Prince and the Pauper* (1882), and *Life on the Mississippi* (1883). My later works include: *A Connecticut Yankee in King Arthur's Court* (1889), *Tom Sawyer Abroad* (1893), and *Personal Recollections of Joan of Arc* (1896), which I believe to be my greatest work, but the critics hated it.

I was born Samuel Langhorne Clemens on November 30, 1835, in Florida, Missouri, but spent my boyhood in Hannibal, Missouri. At the age of 18, I worked for my brother Orion's newspaper as an apprentice printer. Here I began writing juvenile stories and humorous sketches. For the next ten years (1853–1862), I wrote various humorous sketches under various pen names. In 1862, I took a job as a reporter and humorist for the Virginia City *Territorial Enterprise*. The following year, I changed my name and began to write books and humorous sketches. I wrote my last words on April 21, 1910, in Redding, Connecticut. My last work, *The Mysterious Stranger* (1916) was published after my death.

WHO AM I?

1. I was born on November 30, 1835, in Florida, Missouri.
2. At the age of 18, I worked for my brother Orion's newspaper as an apprentice printer.
3. My first novel, *The Gilded Age* (1873), was written in collaboration with Charles Dudley Warner.
4. My other works include: "The Celebrated Jumping Frog of Calaveras County" (1865), *The Prince and the Pauper* (1883), and *A Connecticut Yankee in King Arthur's Court* (1889).
5. *The Adventures of Tom Sawyer* (1876) and *The Adventures of Huckleberry Finn* (1884) were my most successful works.

8

When people hear my name, they think of my novels about life in China. My first novel about China was *East Wind, West Wind* (1930). I followed that up with *The Good Earth* (1931), which won international attention and a Pulitzer Prize in 1932. To complete the trilogy, I wrote *Sons* (1932) and *A House Divided* (1935), which were published together in *The House of Earth* (1935). My other works include: *The Mother* (1934); *Fighting Angel* (1936) and *The Exile* (1936), both of which contributed to my Nobel Prize in literature (1938); and *Today and Forever* (1941). My later works include: *The Hidden Flower* (1952), the autobiographies *My Several Worlds* (1954) and *A Bridge for Passing* (1962), and *All Under Heaven* (1973). I died on March 6, 1973, in Danby, Vermont.

I was born on June 26, 1892, in Hillsboro, West Virginia. My mother was the driving force behind my interest in writing. Each day she would give me writing exercises and encourage me to submit my writings for publication.

My first writings were published in the *Shanghai Mercury* (my parents were missionaries to China at the time). After being educated in Shanghai, I returned to the United States (at the age of 17) to attend Randolph-Macon Women's College in Virginia. My years at Randolph were fruitful; I wrote many stories and poems, and one school play. I also won two literary awards for my writing. In 1925, I attended Cornell University, where I earned an M.A. in English (1926). Sometimes I worked under the pen name of John Sedges.

WHO AM I?

1. I was born on June 26, 1892, in Hillsboro, West Virginia.
2. Sometimes I worked under the pen name of John Sedges.
3. My first writings were published in the *Shanghai Mercury*.
4. My books, *Fighting Angel* (1936) and *The Exile* (1936) contributed to my 1938 Nobel Prize in literature.
5. I am best remembered for my books about China, such as *East Wind, West Wind* (1930), *The Good Earth* (1931), *Sons* (1932), and *A House Divided* (1935).

During the 1920s, my success as a writer flourished with the publication of five very successful novels. These novels included: *Main Street* (1920), my first success which was originally called *The Village Virus*; *Babbitt* (1922); *Arrowsmith* (1925); *Elmer Gantry* (1927), and *Dodsworth* (1929). The following year, I won the Nobel Prize for literature (1930), becoming the first American to win such an award.

My other works include: *Mantrap* (1926), *Ann Vickers* (1933), *It Can't Happen Here* (1935), *The Prodigal Parents* (1938), *Kingsblood Royal* (1947), *The God-Seekers* (1949), and *World So Wide* (1951). After the success of *Main Street* I began to drink heavily, which contributed to my death on January 10, 1951, in Rome, Italy.

I was born on February 7, 1885, in Sauk Centre, Minnesota. After a disappointing childhood I left my hometown (at the age of 17) to study at the Oberlin Academy, where I prepared for my entrance to Yale College. It was at Yale that I decided to devote my life to writing and began writing prose and verse for college magazines. Feeling confident my senior year, I left school to pursue a career as a freelance writer. This field proved fruitless, so I returned to Yale and graduated in 1908. For the next seven years, I held various journalistic jobs; I worked in a New York publishing firm for five of those years. My career began to take off with the publication of my first novel, *Our Mr. Wrenn: The Romantic Adventure of a Gentle Man* (1914).

WHO AM I?

1. I was born on February 7, 1885, in Sauk Centre, Minnesota.
2. In 1930, I won the Nobel Prize for literature, the first American to win such an award.
3. My career began to take off with the publication of my first novel, *Our Mr. Wrenn: The Romantic Adventure of a Gentle Man* (1914).
4. I declined the Pulitzer Prize for my book *Arrowsmith* (1925).
5. My most successful books include: *Main Street* (1920), *Babbitt* (1922), *Elmer Gantry* (1927), and *Dodsworth* (1928).

10

Most of my books and short stories took place in fictional Yoknapatawpha County, Mississippi. These books include: *The Sound and the Fury* (1929), *As I Lay Dying* (1930), and *Light in August* (1932). My most impressive work was my masterpiece *Absalom, Absalom!* (1936). I gained most of my recognition in my later years, when I received the Nobel Prize (1949), the National Book Award (1951), and two Pulitzer Prizes in literature (1955 and 1963). My work during this period includes: *Knight's Gambit* (1949), *Requiem for a Nun* (1951), and *The Mansion* (1959), which completed my "Snopes" trilogy. My last novel *The Reivers* (1962) was published before my death on July 6, 1962, in Oxford, Mississippi.

I was born on September 25, 1897, in New Albany, Mississippi. At the age of 16, I became interested in poetry. Later, after spending a few dismal months as a clerk in the book department of Lord and Taylor, I returned to Mississippi to become postmaster of a university. After two years I was fired for reading on the job. In 1919, I published my first poem "L' Ápres Midi d'un Faune." My first book was a collection of poems called *The Marble Faun* (1924). Two years later while living in New Orleans, my second book, *Soldier's Pay* (1926), was given rave reviews by the critics, but sold sparingly. My later works include: *The Unvanquished* (1938); *Go Down, Moses* (1942), the first in the "Snopes" trilogy; and *Intruder in the Dust* (1948).

WHO AM I?

1. I was born on September 25, 1897, in New Albany, Mississippi.
2. My first book was a collection of poems called *The Marble Faun* (1924).
3. I received the Nobel Prize (1949) and two Pulitzer Prizes in literature (1955 and 1963).
4. My later works include: *Knight's Gambit* (1949), *Requiem for a Nun* (1951), and *The Mansion* (1959).
5. My most impressive work was the masterpiece, *Absalom, Absalom!* (1936).

My *Little Women* series told the story of the March family; Meg, Jo, Beth, and Amy. It also brought me enormous success and notoriety as a writer. My first volume of *Little Women* was published in 1868, with a second volume in 1869. Two years later, I wrote its sequel, *Little Men* (1871). Some of my other works include: *Moods* (1864), *An Old Fashioned Girl* (1870), and *Shawl Straps: Aunt Jo's Scrapbag, II* (1872). My later works include: *Eight Cousins* (1875), *Under the Lilacs* (1879), *Spinning-Wheel Stories* (1884), and *Jo's Boys and How They Turned Out: A Sequel to Little Men* (1886). My celebrated life of a writer ended on March 6, 1888, in Boston, Massachusetts.

I was born on November 29, 1832, in Germantown, Pennsylvania. My parents pushed me into writing because of my talent and creativity. They even enlisted the help of their friends, Ralph Waldo Emerson and Henry David Thoreau. Under their direction, I published poetry under the pen name of Flora Fairfield. My first book, *Flower Fables* (1854), was a collection of short stories. Soon my poems and short stories began showing up in magazines. My next book, *Hospital Sketches* (1863), was a collection of letters that I sent home to my family while serving as a nurse at Union Hospital (Washington, DC) during the Civil War.

WHO AM I?

1. I was born on November 29, 1832, in Germantown, Pennsylvania.
2. With the help of Ralph Waldo Emerson and Henry David Thoreau, I published poetry under the pen name Flora Fairfield.

3. My first book, *Flower Fables* (1854), was a collection of short stories.
4. My later works include: *Eight Cousins* (1875), *Under the Lilacs* (1879), and *Spinning-Wheel Stories* (1884).
5. My *Little Women* series told of the March family (Meg, Jo, Beth, and Amy), in such books as *Little Women* (1868), *Little Men* (1871), and *Jo's Boys and How They Turned Out: A Sequel to Little Men* (1886).

12

My fourth book, *Nobody Knows My Name* (1957), thrust me into the spotlight of contemporary American literature. Previously I had gained critical acclaim for my books *Go Tell It on the Mountain* (1953) and *Notes of a Native Son* (1955), but book sales were minimal at best. Then I struck good fortune again with my novel *Another Country* (1962), which was a success with the critics and public alike. My next book, *The Fire Next Time* (1963), was an instant best-seller. I was flying high as the most quoted black author of the decade. My later books include: *Going to Meet the Man* (1965), *Tell Me How Long the Train's Been Gone* (1968), and *No Name in the Street* (1972).

I was born on August 2, 1924, in New York City, New York. My father was a strict, religious man who wanted me to become a preacher. At the age of 14, I fulfilled his wishes by preaching at storefront churches in Harlem, New York. But when I attended De Witt Clinton High School and served as editor of the school magazine, my attentions turned toward writing. My father was not thrilled with my decision, so I left home at 17. Three years later, I won the Eugene Saxton Fellowship, and was able to pursue my writing full-time. I went on to write several books and two mildly successful plays that made it to the New York stage: *Blues for Master Charlie* (1964) and *The Amen Corner* (1968).

WHO AM I?

1. I was born on August 2, 1924, in New York City, New York.
2. At the age of 14, I fulfilled my father's wishes by preaching at storefront churches in Harlem, New York.
3. When I was 20, I won the Eugene Saxton Fellowship, and was able to pursue my writing full-time.

4. I gained critical acclaim for my books *Go Tell It on the Mountain* (1953) and *Notes of a Native Son* (1955).
5. *Nobody Knows My Name* (1957), *Another Country* (1962), and *The Fire Next Time* (1963) were my most successful books.

Chapter Seven

Inventors

1

My invention of the cotton gin revolutionized the cotton industry in the South; no longer did the cotton have to be slowly picked by hand. Instead, one machine could clean up to 50 pounds of cotton per day. The gin itself was a wooden cylinder with rows of tiny metal spikes and a revolving brush that cleaned the cotton from the spikes. In the process the tightly clinging cotton seeds were separated from the cotton and dropped into a smaller container. I first demonstrated the machine in April 1793, and obtained a patent for it on March 14, 1794. In 1798, I obtained a two-year government contract to produce 10,000 guns against the threat of war with France. At the Mill Rock shop where we made the guns, the first assembly line was born; we used interchangeable parts.

I was born on December 8, 1765, in Westboro, Massachusetts. When I was about 15 or 16 (at the time of the American Revolution), it was difficult to purchase nails and other goods, so I filled the need and earned financial success from a workshop I built on the family farm. After earning enough money for a college education, I left the farm at 19 to pursue a degree in law. As a way to earn spending money, I made and repaired various mechanical pieces. After graduating from Yale in 1792, I went to Savannah, Georgia, to work as a tutor. There I met the widow of General Nathanael Greene, who persuaded me to invent a machine that could clean cotton. I was inducted into the Inventors Hall of Fame in 1900.

WHO AM I?

1. I was born on December 8, 1765, in Westboro, Massachusetts.

2. I graduated from Yale in 1792 with a degree in law.
3. I was inducted into the Inventors Hall of Fame in 1900.
4. In 1798, I created a system of interchangeable parts for firearms.
5. I invented the cotton gin in 1793 (patented in 1794).

2

My inventive mind produced 1,069 patents, of which the incandescent light bulb and the phonograph were my best known. My first success with the light bulb (using a thin carbon filament) came on October 19, 1879, when it burned for 45 hours without overheating. After experimenting with over 6,000 other organic materials, I was able to come up with a light bulb that could burn up to 1,000 hours using a bamboo fiber. Earlier in 1869, I began experimenting with the electrical transmission of the human voice. By 1876, I obtained a patent for an electric transmitter system. A year later, I moved my laboratory to Menlo Park, where I invented the phonograph and became the first to record sound (1877). In 1888, I invented a high-speed camera and kinetograph for the film industry.

I was born on February 11, 1847, in Milan, Ohio. My family moved to Michigan, where I set up a basement laboratory in our home when I was ten years old. Two years later, to help support my family, I found a job on a train selling candy and newspapers. Within three years, I was promoted to telegraph operator. At the age of 19, I took out my first patent for an electric vote recorder (1866). This invention led to my first big success, the "ticker," a tape machine that recorded up-to-date stock exchange prices. The Gold & Stock Telegraph Co. bought the rights to the "ticker" and my other telegraph improvements for $30,000. In 1869, I quit my job and used the money to start a research laboratory in Newark, New Jersey. I died on October 18, 1931 (at the age of 84), in West Orange, New Jersey.

WHO AM I?

1. I was born on February 11, 1847, in Milan, Ohio.
2. At the age of 12, I worked as a train-boy on the Grand Trunk Railroad, selling candy and newspapers.

3. My first big success was the "ticker," a tape machine that recorded up-to-date stock exchange prices.
4. At my Menlo Park laboratory, I invented the phonograph and became the first to record sound (1877).
5. My first success with the incandescent light bulb came on October 19, 1879, when it burned for 45 hours.

3 My most successful invention, the vulcanization of rubber, happened simply by accident on top of a hot stove. As I was mixing sulphur and various other ingredients, I spilled some of the mixture on the stove. I left it overnight, and when it had cooled the next morning, the rubber had vulcanized. In 1836, I thought I had found a solution to the problem of rubber staying strong at high temperatures; I added nitric acid to the raw rubber to keep it strong. The process proved unsuccessful in the use of mail bags, however, and I was forced to go back to the drawing board. The following year I purchased Nathaniel Hayward's process of adding sulphur to raw rubber. By 1844, I had successfully perfected the process and obtained a patent.

I was born on December 29, 1800, in New Haven, Connecticut. My first interest in inventing came when I worked for my father's hardware business in Naugatuck. Here I invented many farm implements, including a lightweight steel pitchfork. By 1830, the business was in serious financial trouble and I had to find other work. After the success of my best-known invention, many of my patents were stolen by several of my associates. By 1855, my debts had mounted and I was jailed in Paris for those debts. I died a broken man on July 1, 1860, in New York City, New York, still heavily burdened by debt.

WHO AM I?

1. I was born on December 29, 1800, in New Haven, Connecticut.
2. My first interest in inventing came when I worked in my father's hardware business in Naugatuck.
3. I spent time in a debtors' prison in Paris, while others became rich off my invention.
4. My first attempt at rubber mail bags was unsuccessful.
5. By 1844, I had successfully perfected the vulcanization of rubber and obtained a patent.

My two-paddle wheel steamboat, the *Clermont*, was one of the first successful steamboats built. It made its maiden voyage up the Hudson River in 1807. The 100-foot hull was fitted with a 24 horsepower engine that could travel 5 miles-per-hour. Earlier in 1803, my partner (Robert Livingstone) and I had obtained a steam engine from a British company, which we installed in ships made in New York. While living in France, I began experimenting with steam engines and how they could be used to power ships. Earlier, I had applied these same principles to the *Nautilus* (a submarine). These experiments led to the steam-powered warship I built for the United States Navy in 1815.

I was born on November 14, 1765, in Lancaster County, Pennsylvania. At a young age, I showed promise as an artist and was employed by a gunsmith to draw designs. As early as the age of 14, I had made my first designs of a small paddleboat. When I was 17, I moved to Philadelphia and worked as a portrait painter for four years. In 1786, I traveled to London, England, to study under the direction of Benjamin West. Here, under the influence of the Industrial Revolution, I turned my attentions toward engineering and engineering projects. I also obtained patents for a mechanical canal dredger, a canal boat hauling device, a spinning flax machine, a marble shaving machine, and a rope twisting machine. I died on February 24, 1815, in New York City, New York.

WHO AM I?

1. I was born on November 14, 1765, in Lancaster County, Pennsylvania.
2. In 1786, I traveled to London, England, to study under the direction of Benjamin West.
3. My patents include: a mechanical canal dredger, a spinning flax machine, and a marble shaving machine.
4. In 1800, I launched the submarine *Nautilus.*
5. My two-paddle wheel steamboat, the *Clermont,* was one of the first successful steamboats built.

5

With the production of my horseless carriage, the Model T, and the introduction of the assembly line, the world was pulled out of the doldrums of the Industrial Revolution, and into a new era of confidence and hope. My rise in fame and fortune began on June 16, 1903, when I founded the Ford Motor Company. Our first automobile sold was the Model N (built in 1896), a low-priced car that sold immediately and rapidly. With the success of the Model N, I began offering the Model T in 1908. It came equipped with a four-cylinder, 20 horsepower engine, and was offered in only one color—black. We sold 15 million models over the next 19 years. In 1928, I offered a new design in the Model A. It was available in four colors and 17 body styles, with a V-8 engine and safety glass windshields (first automobile to have such a feature) as standard equipment. I remained as president of the company until 1945. I died on April 7, 1947, in Dearborn, Michigan.

I was born on July 30, 1863, in Springwells, Michigan. At an early age,

I showed an aptitude for mechanical ability and inventiveness. When I moved to Detroit at the age of 16, I found work as a machinist's apprentice. After work I kept busy repairing watches and clocks. When I completed my apprenticeship, I went to work on Westinghouse steam engines. Then I moved on to the Edison Illuminating Company as a chief engineer in 1891. Two years later, I designed a one-cylinder gasoline engine. In 1899, I resigned and joined the Detroit Automobile Company. Four years later, I left to start my own company, determined to build a reputation in the race car business.

WHO AM I?

1. I was born on July 30, 1863, in Springwells, Michigan.

2. In 1891, I became a chief engineer for the Edison Illuminating Company.
3. I built race cars and became a well-known race car driver.
4. In 1903, I started the Ford Motor Company with $100,000.
5. I introduced the Model T in 1908, which was produced on a moving assembly line beginning in 1913.

I was able to develop over 800 varieties of fruits, vegetables, grains, flowers, ornamentals, and grasses through the use of hybridization and selection. My first success came with the development of the Idaho potato (also called the Burbank potato), which allowed me to move to Santa Rosa, California, in 1875. Here I bought a four-acre plot for a garden and greenhouse and an eight-acre tract to grow a variety of plants.

Through my various experiments, I discovered that the environment and heredity had the most effect on the growth and development of individual plants. By modifying the heredity of the plants, I discovered the process of hybridization (the cross-pollination of plants of various varieties to produce new varieties). This process resulted in offspring that were superior to their parents.

My life began on March 7, 1849, in Lancaster, Massachusetts. My interest in plants began at an early age on my family's farm. By the time I was 21, I had earned enough money to buy a 17-acre farm in Lunenberg, Massachusetts.

One day while working the soil, I discovered a potato seedball and planted them individually into the soil. Each seed produced one plant, but I only kept four because they produced plants that were superior. This discovery led to the techniques of hybridization and selection, which I carried out on a large scale. With my experiments on plums alone, I produced 30,000 new varieties, which resulted in the selection of 113 superior varieties.

WHO AM I?

1. I was born on March 7, 1849, in Lancaster, Massachusetts.

2. By the time I was 21, I had earned enough money to buy a 17-acre farm in Lunenberg, Massachusetts.
3. In 1875, I bought a four-acre plot for a garden and greenhouse and an eight-acre tract to grow a variety of plants. Both pieces of land were in Santa Rosa, California.
4. By modifying the heredity of the plants, I discovered the process of hybridization (the cross-pollination of plants of various varieties to produce new varieties).
5. I was able to develop over 800 varieties of fruits, vegetables, grains, flowers, ornamentals, and grasses; my most famous was the Idaho potato (also called the Burbank potato).

On December 17, 1903, at Kitty Hawk, North Carolina, my brother made the first motorized airplane flight (120 feet). I made the longest flight of the day, 852 feet in 59 seconds. Earlier, in 1899, we had attempted to fly a glider at Kitty Hawk (one of the windiest places in the country) and failed. Deciding to give it one more try, we took the glider to nearby Kill Devil Hill, where we made many successful glides down the side of the hill. Still dismayed about the glider's lifting ability, we began testing various wing surfaces and angles (over 200 types). Our 1902 glider had a larger wing span (32 feet), which allowed us to make glides of over 600 feet. The following year, we added a motor of our own design. In 1905, after making further adjustments, I flew 24 miles over a field near Dayton, Ohio. Three years later, we signed a contract with the United States War Department to supply them with army planes.

I was born on April 16, 1867, in Millville, Indiana; my brother was born on August 19, 1871, in Dayton, Ohio. As children we were interested in flying toy helicopters (powered by rubber bands) and the aerodynamics associated with it. In 1889, we began printing the *West Side News* on a home-made printing press of our own design. Four years later, we opened a bicycle repair shop and manufactured our own bicycles. Then our interest in aerodynamics was aroused once again with news of Otto Lilienthal's death. We had closely followed his experiments with gliders and were ready to step in where his experiments ended. It was my idea to use sideways balance, a method of presenting each wing at different angles to the wind. I accomplished this balance by twisting or warping the wings to the precise angle determined to be the best aerodynamically. In July 1899, we built a small kite-like glider to test this method, which proved successful.

WHO AM I?

1. I was born on April 16, 1867, in Millville, Indiana; my brother was born on August 19, 1871, in Dayton, Ohio.
2. In 1889, we began printing the *West Side News* on a homemade press of our own design.
3. Four years later, we opened a bicycle repair shop and manufactured our own bicycles.

4. In 1899, we made many successful glides at Kill Devil Hill, North Carolina, with our glider.
5. On December 17, 1903, at Kitty Hawk, North Carolina, my brother made the first motorized airplane flight (120 feet). I made the longest flight of the day: 852 feet.

8 In 1888, I began selling my Kodak camera, which included shoulder strap and case, to the public for $25. The camera's stripping film roll had 100 exposures, and for it to be developed the whole camera had to be sent back to our factory in Rochester, New York. For a $10 fee we developed the film and loaded it with a fresh roll of film. Later, I began spooling my film, so it would not have to be sent back to the factory. The spooling also allowed for daylight loading, which popularized amateur photography. By 1900, I began manufacturing a pocket-sized camera for only $1. Others tried to copy my camera, but my invention of transparent nitrocellulose roll film kept me on top for three decades.

I was born on July 12, 1854, in Waterville, New York. At the age of 14, I left school to work as a messenger boy to help support my family. In the evening I studied accounting, but soon turned my attentions to photography. I began experimenting with photographic emulsions in 1878. The following year, I obtained a patent for a photographic emulsion coating machine (1879). In 1880, I began mass-producing dry plates in a rented loft in Rochester, New York. Despite all my commercial successes in the marketplace, my personal problems were so great that I committed suicide on March 14, 1932.

WHO AM I?

1. I was born on July 12, 1854, in Waterville, New York.
2. In 1880, I began mass-producing dry plates in a rented loft in Rochester, New York.
3. I began experimenting with photographic emulsions in 1878.
4. By 1900, I began manufacturing a pocket-sized camera for only $1.
5. In 1888, I began selling my Kodak camera with 100 exposures.

9

I traveled the country giving demonstrations of laughing gas (nitrous oxide) to earn enough money to build my prototype revolver, which I perfected in 1835. This same year, I obtained a patent for my revolver in England and France. The following year, I obtained a patent in the United States. To manufacture my five-shooter revolver, I built a factory in Paterson, New Jersey, called the Patent Arms Manufacturing Company. The factory also produced various rifles and shotguns. My company failed in 1842, due to consumers' dissatisfaction with earlier made firearms, but with the outbreak of the Mexican-American War (1846), I was back in business. The United States government ordered 1,000 revolvers that year, providing me with enough profits to build an armory in Hartford, Connecticut (the largest of its kind). Here I manufactured the .44 caliber revolver (1835), .31 caliber Pocket Model (1848), .36 caliber Colt Navy (1851, my most famous revolver), the Rootes .28 caliber (1860), the Army (1860), and the Police Model (1862). With the success of these firearms, I died a wealthy man on January 10, 1862, in Hartford, Connecticut.

My life began on July 19, 1814, in Hartford, Connecticut. I knew at an early age that I wanted to be an inventor. One of my first inventions was a four-barrel rifle, which had problems of reliability. Through my experiments with gunpowder, I discovered that gunpowder could be fired with an electrical current. I used this knowledge to invent an explosive mine that proved disastrous at its first public demonstration: it covered the spectators in mud. My parents then sent me off to Amherst Academy. Here my troubles continued when one of my experiments caused a fire and school officials asked me to leave. Hoping the sea would change my fortunes, I became an apprenticed seaman. In 1830, during one of my journeys at sea, I discovered that the helmsman's wheel rotation could be applied to firearms. This discovery prompted me to leave the sea (at the age of 18) to follow my dreams.

WHO AM I?

1. My life began on July 19, 1814, in Hartford, Connecticut.
2. At the Amherst Academy, one of my experiments caused a fire and school officials asked me to leave.

3. I traveled the country giving demonstrations of laughing gas (nitrous oxide).
4. I manufactured my five-shooter revolver at the Patent Arms Manufacturing Company in Paterson, New Jersey.
5. My most famous revolver was the .36 caliber Colt Navy (1851).

10

I am best remembered for my famous kite-flying experiment (1751), which proved that lightning was a form of electricity. Through this discovery, I began making lightning rods that soon graced buildings all over the world. My other scientific discoveries and inventions include: measurement of the Gulf Stream, tracking storm patterns, heat absorption, ship designs, the printing press, a student desk, an electrostatic generator, bifocal lenses, the harmonica, and the most famous — the Pennsylvania fireplace, or stove (which was later named after me). For my efforts, I was inducted into the Royal Society (1756) in England and the French Academy of Sciences (1772). I also gained enormous popularity for writing *Poor Richard's Almanack*, which I wrote while publishing a Philadelphia newspaper.

I was born on January 17, 1706, in Boston, Massachusetts. My early years were spent in poverty, without much of a formal education. I had thoughts of entering the ministry, but my attentions turned to my brother's newspaper, the *New England Courant* (Boston). Here I worked as an apprentice printer for about five years. At the age of 17, I ran away to Philadelphia to publish my own newspaper, the *Pennsylvania Gazette*. After a successful career as a scientist, I turned to politics and public service. This public career began in the Pennsylvania Assembly (1751), included being a member of the Constitutional Convention, and which spanned almost 40 years.

WHO AM I?

1. I was born on January 17, 1706, in Boston, Massachusetts.
2. At the age of 17, I ran away to Philadelphia to publish my own newspaper, the *Pennsylvania Gazette*.
3. My career in politics began in the Pennsylvania Assembly (1751),

continued as a member of the Constitutional Convention, and it spanned almost 40 years.

4. Some of my inventions include: the printing press, the student desk, the electrostatic generator, bifocal lenses, and the Pennsylvania fireplace.

5. I am best remembered for my famous kite-flying experiment (1751) and *Poor Richard's Almanack.*

Most of my life was spent developing the sewing machine. I first began working on the sewing machine around 1843. By the following year, I had developed a rough working model. In September 1846, I obtained a United States patent for the machine. The machine featured a locking stitch mechanism (the first to have such a device), an under-thread shuttle, and a curved needle with an eye. That same year, I sold my invention to a corset manufacturer in England for 250 pounds. I had also pawned off my patent rights in the United States. Later, when I returned to the United States, I found that the sewing machine had gained in its popularity and others were taking advantage of my patent; one such inventor was Isaac Singer.

I was born on July 9, 1819, in Spencer, Massachusetts. At an early age, I took an interest in machinery, both at the grist and sawmills where I worked. Here I apprenticed as a machinist and began developing my idea for a sewing machine. After a disappointing career in London I returned to the United States in poverty with my wife near death. Seeing that my patent had been infringed upon, I went to court to sue the inventors for their infringements. I won the case, retrieved my patent rights, and was awarded royalties off of all the sewing machines made in the United States until the expiration of my patent (1852–1867).

WHO AM I?

1. I was born on July 9, 1819, in Spencer, Massachusetts.

2. At an early age, I took an interest in machinery and apprenticed as a machinist.

3. I sold my invention to a corset manufacturer in England for 250 pounds.

4. By 1846, I obtained a United States patent for my machine that featured a locking stitch mechanism.
5. I first began working on the sewing machine in 1843.

12

The business I established in 1838 with my partner, Major Leonard Andrus, led to an international company that uses a deer and the color green as its trademarks. That year, we designed three plows with a steel share and a wrought iron moldboard. Later, I began making the moldboards out of steel and adjusted the curvature to meet the demands of various soil types. The plow was so successful that beginning in 1846 we sold a thousand plows per year. Eager to strike out on my own, I sold my interest to Andrus and started a plow business (bears my name today) in Moline, Illinois. Here I began manufacturing plows with the first domestic-cast plow steel (Pittsburgh, Pennsylvania), which resulted in an output of 13,000 plows in 1858.

I was born on February 7, 1804, in Rutland, Vermont. At an early age I became interested in the blacksmith trade and later served a four-year apprenticeship. I worked as a blacksmith in my hometown until 1837, then moved to Detour, Illinois, where I continued in the trade. Here I specialized in farm implements and learned from the farmers that the plows currently being used were too heavy (made of cast iron) and ineffective (unable to turn the soil of the prairie). This discovery led to the design of my lightweight plow and a company that still operates today (over 150 years later). I died on May 17, 1886, in Moline, Illinois.

WHO AM I?

1. I was born on February 7, 1804, in Rutland, Vermont.
2. At an early age I became interested in the blacksmith trade and later served a four-year apprenticeship.
3. In Detour, Illinois, I specialized in farm implements.
4. In 1858, I manufactured 13,000 plows made of domestic-cast plow steel (the first to be made of this material).
5. The business I established in 1838 still uses a deer and the color green as its trademarks.

Chapter Eight

Musicians/Composers

1

I am best remembered for my masterpiece *Kiss Me, Kate* (1948), a musical play that spawned eight popular songs. My best-known songs include: "Let's Do It (Let's Fall in Love)" (1928), "Night and Day" (1932), "You're the Top" (1934), "I Get a Kick Out of You" (1934), "Don't Fence Me In" (1934), and "It's De-lovely" (1936). I also wrote several songs for Hollywood films, such as *The Gay Divorcee* (1934), *Anything Goes* (1936), *Born to Dance* (1936), *Rosalie* (1937), and *High Society* (1956). I first achieved success with the musical shows *Wake Up and Dream* (London stage) and *50 Million Frenchmen* (New York stage), both in 1929. My later musicals were not so successful, except for *Can-can* (1953). A film biography of my sons (including 14 of my most popular songs) called *Night and Day* was made in 1946. I died on October 15, 1964, in Santa Monica, California.

My life began on June 9, 1892, in Peru, Indiana. My mother (a pianist in her own right) was instrumental in having me take violin lessons at the age of six and piano lessons at the age of eight at the Marion Conservatory. While attending the Worcester Academy (1905–1909) in Massachusetts, I began writing melodies. My first published work, "The Bobolink Waltz" (1902) led to other melodies for amateur shows. I also wrote songs ("Bingo Eli Yale" and "Bulldog," two popular football songs) for the Dramatic Club at Yale University (1909–1913), along with conducting and singing with the university glee club. After graduation I attended Harvard University (1915–1916) to study harmony and counterpoint. My first Broadway show, *See America First* (1916), was a failure, but I pressed on and did not let this setback be a discouragement to me.

WHO AM I?

1. I was born on June 9, 1892, in Peru, Indiana.
2. While attending the Worcester Academy (1905–1909) in Massachusetts, I began writing melodies.
3. At Yale University, I wrote two famous football songs ("Bingo Eli Yale" and "Bulldog") for the Dramatic Club.
4. Some of my best-known songs include: "Let's Do It (Let's Fall in Love)" (1928), "You're the Top" (1934), and "Don't Fence Me In" (1934).
5. I am best remembered for my masterpiece *Kiss Me, Kate* (1948), a musical play that spawned eight popular songs.

2

My most impressive musical, *West Side Story* (1957), brought me international success. Most baby boomers will remember me for my television appearances as conductor and introducer of young people's concerts. Earlier, my composition "First Symphony" (1944) brought me a New York Music Critics' Circle Award. That same year, the success of my first ballet, *Fancy Free*, led to a full-production Broadway musical called *On the Town* (1944). It successfully ran for 463 performances, which paved the way for other musicals.

My other works include: the ballet *Facsimile* (1946), music for *Peter Pan* (1950), the musical *Wonderful Town* (1952), and the film score for *On the Waterfront* (1954). In recognition of my work, I was asked to write a dedication for the opening of the JFK Center for the Performing Arts (opened September 1971, in Washington, DC); the dramatic work was titled "Mass."

I was born on August 25, 1918, in Lawrence, Massachusetts. At the age of ten, I began taking piano lessons. I continued my study of the piano at Harvard University. After graduating in 1939, I studied piano, orchestration, and conducting at the Curtis Institute. It was here that I gained a fondness for conducting, and for the next two summers I studied at Tanglewood. Shortly after leaving Curtis, I wrote and published my first composition, "The Clarinet Sonata." This work led to a position with the New York Philharmonic Orchestra as an assistant conductor. The concert (November 13, 1944) was such a big hit that it launched my conducting career. This concert led to other conducting positions: New York City Orchestra (1945–1948), the Israel Philharmonic Orchestra (1947–1949), head of Tanglewood's Conducting Department (1951–1955), and a return to the New York Philharmonic (1957–1969), where I was honored as lifetime laureate conductor.

WHO AM I?

1. I was born on August 25, 1918, in Lawrence, Massachusetts.
2. After graduating from Harvard in 1939, I studied piano, orchestration, and conducting at the Curtis Institute.
3. In 1944, the success of my first ballet, *Fancy Free*, led to a full-production Broadway musical called *On the Town*.
4. I wrote the music for *Peter Pan* (1950), the film score for *On the Waterfront* (1954), and conducted the New York Philharmonic Orchestra for many years.
5. My most impressive musical, *West Side Story* (1957), brought me international success.

3 I wrote the scripts or lyrics for more than 30 shows and films. My most memorable hits include: *Oklahoma!* (1943), *South Pacific* (1949), *The King and I* (1951), *Flower Drum Song* (1958), and *The Sound of Music* (1959); all were written with my very talented partner Richard Rodgers, with whom I first teamed on Broadway with the non-musical play *I Remember Mama* (1944). We will long be remembered for our songs from *Oklahoma*: "Oh! What a Beautiful Mornin'," "People Will Say We're in Love," and "The Surrey with the Fringe on Top." Other smash hits include: *Wildflower* (my first hit show, 1923), *Rose-Marie* (1924), *The Desert Song* (1926), and *Showboat* (1927). I am also known for the popular songs for which I wrote the lyrics: "Ol' Man River" (1927), "Make Believe" (1927), and "The Last Time I Saw Paris" (1940). My career ended on August 23, 1960, in Doylestown, Pennsylvania.

My life began on July 12, 1895, in New York City, New York. My early interests did not involve music because I wanted to pursue a different career from my family (three generations; grandfather, father, uncle's son). I earned a B.A. (1916) from Columbia and entered their law school. While

attending Columbia, I became involved with the stage and joined the Columbia University Players Club. I enjoyed these student performances, especially my comedic part in *On Your Way* and my leading role in *The Peace Pirates*. This experience encouraged me to write a Shakespearean skit and a book, and lyrics for the school production *Home, James*, which I also acted in. I worked briefly in a law office before completely turning my attentions to the stage.

WHO AM I?

1. My life began on July 12, 1895, in New York City, New York.
2. In 1916, I earned a B.A. from Columbia and entered their law school.
3. My popular songs include: "Ol' Man River" (1927), "Make Believe" (1927), and "The Last Time I Saw Paris" (1940).

4. Other smash hits include: *Wildflower* (1923), *Rose-Marie* (1924), *The Desert Song* (1926), and *Showboat* (1927).
5. My most memorable hits include: *Oklahoma!* (1943), *South Pacific* (1949), *The King and I* (1951), *Flower Drum Song* (1958), and *The Sound of Music* (1959).

4   My first great success came in 1920, when Al Jolson recorded my song "Swanee" (1919), which sold hundreds of thousands of copies. My successes continued with such hits as "Lady Be Good" (1924), "Rhapsody in Blue" (1924), "Strike Up the Band" (1927), "An American in Paris" (1928), and "Porgy and Bess" (1934–1935). Then in 1932, my musical *Of Thee I Sing* (1931) was honored with the Pulitzer Prize in drama (first musical to be so honored). I teamed with my brother Ira to become one of Broadway's most successful teams, with such songs as "The Man I Love" (1924), "How Long Has This Been Going On?" (1927), "Rosalie" (1928), and "Til Then" (1933). I also found success with the Hollywood films *Shall We Dance* (1936–1937), *A Damsel in Distress* (1937), and *Kiss Me, Stupid* (1964). I died on July 11, 1937, in Hollywood, California, during an operation to remove a brain tumor.

I was born on September 26, 1898, in Brooklyn, New York. Growing up on Manhattan's east side in a poor Jewish community, I had little opportunity to hear music. Instead, I spent time playing various sports in the streets until my parents brought home an upright piano (1910). I quickly learned to play, spending all my free time at the keyboard. Soon I outgrew my neighborhood piano teachers and went to study with Charles Hambitzer (1912). He introduced me to the classics, but failed in teaching me how to read music; I never had that ability.

I left school in 1914 to work at Remick's (a Tin Pan Alley publisher) as a pianist. My first published song, "When You Want 'Em, You Can't Get 'Em, When You Got' Em, You Don't Want 'Em" (1916), led to a successful career on Broadway.

WHO AM I?

1. I was born on September 26, 1898, in Brooklyn, New York.

2. In 1912, I studied with Charles Hambitzer who introduced me to the classics, but failed in teaching me how to read music; I never had the ability.
3. I left school in 1914 to work at Remick's (a Tin Pan Alley publisher) as a pianist.
4. My first great success came in 1920, when Al Jolson recorded my song "Swanee" (1919).
5. The successes continued with "Lady Be Good" (1924), "Rhapsody in Blue" (1924), "Strike Up the Band" (1927), "An American in Paris" (1928), and "Porgy and Bess" (1934–1935).

5

My most successful song, "Old Folks at Home," (1851), was written while under contract to E.P. Christy (whom I let take the credit for the song). During the next 20 years, I wrote approximately 200 songs (of which 135 were for minstrel shows) and 21 hymns and Sunday School songs.

My best-known songs include: "Oh! Susanna" (1848), "Nelly Bly" (1849), "Camptown Races" (1850), "My Old Kentucky Home, Good Night" (1853), and "Jeanie with the Light Brown Hair" (1854).

Two of my songs became official state songs: "My Old Kentucky Home" (Kentucky) and "Old Folks at Home" (Florida). For my efforts, I was inducted into the Hall of Fame for Great Americans (the first musician to be nominated).

I was born on July 4, 1826, in Lawrenceville (now Pittsburgh), Pennsylvania. At an early age my musical talent surfaced, but my parents never encouraged me to pursue it.

Virtually a self-taught musician, I began publishing songs (my first published song was "Open Thy Lattice Love," 1844), while working for my brother as a bookkeeper (1846–1850).

With the success of these songs, I left my brother's employ to become a full-time song-writer. That same year, I signed an exclusive contract with E.P. Christy (a successful minstrel troupe leader) to write songs for his group the Christy's Minstrels. My last song published was "Beautiful Dreamer" (1864); I died on July 13, 1864, in New York City, New York.

WHO AM I?

1. I was born on July 4, 1826, in Lawrenceville, Pennsylvania.
2. Virtually a self-taught musician, I began publishing songs while working for my brother as a bookkeeper (1846–1850).
3. My first published song was "Open Thy Lattice Love" (1844); my last song was "Beautiful Dreamer" (1864).
4. I wrote the song, "Jeanie with the Light Brown Hair" (1854) for my wife Jane Denny McDowell.
5. My best-known songs include: "Oh! Susanna" (1848), "Camptown Races" (1850), and "My Old Kentucky Home" (1853).

6

My most popular morale song, "Over There!" (1917), was popular during both world wars. The songs "(I Am a) Yankee Doodle Boy" (1940) and "Give My Regards to Broadway" (featured in my first non-vaudeville play *Little Johnny Jones,* 1904) also gained popularity.

My other songs include: "Why Did Nellie Leave Home?" (1894), "Hot Tamale Alley" (1895), and "I Guess I'll Have to Telegraph My Baby" (1898). My Broadway works include: *Forty-five Minutes from Broadway* (1906), *The American Idea* (1908), *Hello Broadway* (1914), and *Billie* (1928). I also had success on the stage as an actor in *Ah, Wilderness* (1934) and *I'd Rather Be Right* (1937–1939). The Hollywood film *Yankee Doodle Dandy* (1942) and the Broadway musical *George M* (1969) depicted my life story.

I was born on July 3, 1878, in Providence, Rhode Island. At an early age, I toured with my parents and sister in a vaudeville act (the Four Cohans).

I began writing skits for the act when I was 11 and songs at the age of 13. These experiences led to my first full-length play (three acts), *The Governor's Son* (1901). Two years later, my second play, *Running for Office* (1903), also proved successful for our family's act. For the next 16 years (1904–1920), I worked in partnership with Sam H. Harris on several Broadway shows. Our first play together was *Little Johnny Jones* (1904), a semi-autobiographical work of my life, which spawned other successful works.

WHO AM I?

1. I was born on July 3, 1878, in Providence, Rhode Island.
2. My first full-length play (three acts) was called *The Governor's Son* (1901).
3. The songs "(I Am a) Yankee Doodle Boy" (1904) and "Give My Regards to Broadway" (1904) gained enormous popularity.
4. The Hollywood film *Yankee Doodle Dandy* (1942) and the Broadway show *George M* (1968) depicted my life story.
5. At an early age, I toured with my parents and sister in a vaudeville act (the Four Cohans).

7

The blues made me famous, so it was only fitting that I was given the nickname "Father of the Blues." My career as a composer began in 1909, when I wrote a political campaign song for E.H. "Boss" Crump. The song was originally titled "Mr. Crump," but I later published it as the "Memphis Blues" (1912). Two years later, I published my most famous song, "St. Louis Woman" (also known as "St. Louis Blues," 1914), which was one of America's most popular songs. I followed with the songs: "Yellow Dog Blues" (1914), "Joe Turner Blues" (1915), "Beale Street Blues" (1916), "Careless Love" (1921), and "Aunt Hagar's Blues" (1922). In 1941, my autobiography, *Father of the Blues* (a most appropriate title), was published.

I was born William Christopher on November 16, 1873, in Florence, Alabama. My father was a Methodist minister who believed that all music was of a sinful nature, except for religious hymns. I was so fascinated by music, especially blues, that I left my father's house to go on the road with a minstrel show, playing my cornet. At the age of 25 (after studying at the Kentucky Musical College), I took over as bandleader for the Mahara's Minstrels. I formed two other bands, one in Clarksdale, Mississippi, and one in Memphis, Tennessee (1903). Although I began as a bandleader, my fame was gained from my work as a composer. With failing eyesight, I became a music publisher in New York from the 1920s until my death on March 29, 1958, in New York City, New York.

WHO AM I?

1. I was born William Christopher on November 16, 1873, in Florence, Alabama.
2. My father was a Methodist minsiter who believed that all music was of a sinful nature, except for religious hymns. I was so fascinated by music, especially blues, that I left my father's house to go on the road with a minstrel show.
3. At the age of 25, I took over as bandleader for the Mahara's Minstrels.
4. As a composer I published several songs, including "Memphis Blues" (1912); "St. Louis Woman" (also known as "St. Louis Blues," 1914); my most popular song, "Beale Street Blues" (1916); and "Careless Love" (1921).

5. In 1941, my autobiography, *Father of the Blues* (a most appropriate title), was published.

8

In my lifetime I wrote approximately 70 songs and 136 marches, of which my marches were the most successful. These include "Semper Fidelis" (1888), "The Thunder" (1889), "King Cotton" (1895), "The Stars and Stripes Forever" (1897), "Hands Across the Sea" (1899), and "The Pride of Wolverines" (1926). I also had success with *El Capitan* (operetta, 1896), "The Trooping of the Colors" (pageant, 1898), "The Messiah of Nations" (hymn, 1902), "Showing Off Before Company" (humoresque, 1919), and "The Last Crusada" (ballad, 1920). Some of my songs include: "In Flanders Fields the Poppies Grow" (1918), "Crossing the Bar" (1926), "There's a Merry Brown Thrush" (1926), and "Annabel Lee" (1931). In 1952, the Hollywood film *Stars & Stripes Forever* told the story of my life and career. I was inducted into the Hall of Fame for Great Americans in 1973. I died on March 6, 1932, in Reading, Pennsylvania.

My life began on November 6, 1854, in Washington, DC. I attended local Washington schools and the Esputa Conservatory of Music until I was 13. Then I enlisted in the United States Marine Band (my father was a member) as an apprentice and served for seven years (until I was 20). Here I studied composition, theory, and harmony. This proved useful in my performances on the violin with the Benkert's orchestra and other groups around my hometown. In 1876, I moved to Philadelphia, where I was first violinist in the Offenbach's orchestra. I turned to conducting in 1879 (with *HMS Pinafore*), and a year later I was conducting the variety show *Our Flirtations* (1880). That same year, I rejoined the United States Marine Band as its 14th conductor. I remained in this position until 1892, when I left to form my own band (1892–1931).

WHO AM I?

1. I was born on November 6, 1854, in Washington, DC.
2. I attended the Esputa Conservatory of Music until I was 13, then I enlisted in the United States Marine Band.

3. For my efforts in music, I was inducted into the Hall of Fame for Great Americans in 1973.
4. I gained the most success with my marches, including "Semper Fidelis" (1888), "King Cotton" (1895), and "The Pride of Wolverines" (1926).
5. In 1952, the Hollywood film *Stars and Stripes Forever* told the story of my life and career.

9   My most successful Broadway musical, *The Music Man* (1957), won a Drama Critics' Circle Award and a Tony. It also produced several popular songs, such as "76 Trombones" (1957), which remain classics today. I also had success with two other musicals, *The Unsinkable Molly Brown* (1960) and *Here's Love* (1963). My song "You and I" (1941) remained on top of the Hit Parade for 19 weeks. My other popular songs include: "Gary, Indiana" (1957), "Columbia, The Gem of the Ocean" (1957), and "Belly Up to the Bar, Boy" (1960). Earlier, I wrote the film scores for *The Great Dictator* (1940) and *The Little Foxes* (1941). I also hosted the radio show, *The Big Show* (I wrote the theme song, "May the Good Lord Bless and Keep You," 1950). I died on June 15, 1984, in Santa Monica, California.

I was born on May 18, 1902, in Mason City, Iowa. At a very young age, my mother introduced me to the piano. Soon I mastered the piano and turned to the flute and piccolo. After graduating from Mason City High School (1919), I attended the Institute of Musical Art (later known as Juilliard School of Music). Here I heard that John Philip Sousa was looking for a flutist for his band. I got the job and stayed for a year (1923–1924). Then I joined Hugo Riesenfeld and the Rialto Theatre Orchestra (we played my first composition "Parade Fantastique," 1924). In 1929, I became musical director for the American Broadcasting System (1929–1930). Two years later, I switched over to the National Broadcasting Company (1932–1942), where I directed 17 musical radio shows a week.

WHO AM I?

1. I was born on May 18, 1902, in Mason City, Iowa.
2. While working for the National Broadcasting Company (1932–1942), I directed 17 musical radio shows a week.

3. My first composition was called "Parade Fantastique" (1924).
4. Two of my musicals, *The Unsinkable Molly Brown* (1960) and *Here's Love* (1963), proved very successful.
5. My most successful Broadway musical, *The Music Man* (1957), won a Drama Critics' Circle Award and a Tony.

10

In 1942, I teamed with Frederick Loewe to become part of one of Broadway's most successful tandems. Our most successful musical play, *My Fair Lady* (opened on March 15, 1956, made into a film in 1964), was a box office sensation that grossed $12 million in its first two years. It was also awarded a New York Drama Critics' Circle Award for best musical. We also had enormous success with the musicals *Brigadoon* (1947), which won a New York Drama Critics' Circle Award for best musical and ran for 581 performances, and *Paint Your Wagon* (1951, made into a film in 1969), which ran for 289 performances, and the film *Gigi* (1958). Our final collaboration was *Camelot* (1960). On my own I scored with the play *Love Life* (1948), which ran for 252 performances and was selected as one of the best plays for that year; *Royal Wedding* (1951); *American in Paris* (1951), which won an Academy Award that year; *Brigadoon* (1954); *On a Clear Day You Can See Forever* (1965, made into a film in 1970); and *Coco* (1969).

I was born on August 31, 1918, in New York City, New York. At the age of 11, I decided not to follow my father into his women's apparel business (a national chain of stores that bears our last name). Instead, I began planning a career in the theater by writing and composing music. While enrolled at Harvard, I was active in the Hasty Pudding Club, where I took part in the shows *So Proudly We Hail* (1938) and *Fair Enough* (1939) as a collaborator and singer/dancer. I also spent my summer vacations studying at the Juilliard School of Music. After graduating from Harvard in 1940, I went to work for the Lord and Thomas Agency, writing radio advertising copy. But I left in 1942, to pursue a career as a full-time, freelance writer. During this time I began writing scripts for the radio program *Philco Hall of Fame*.

WHO AM I?

1. I was born on August 31, 1918, in New York City, New York.

2. Instead of following my father into his women's apparel business, I sought a career in the theater.
3. In 1942, I began writing scripts for the radio program *Philco Hall of Fame*.
4. I collaborated on numerous successful musicals, including *Brigadoon* (1947) and *Paint Your Wagon* (1951).
5. Our (Frederick Loewe and myself) most successful musical play, *My Fair Lady*, opened on March 15, 1956.

11

I wrote over 1,000 songs (1932–1952) and made over 20 albums in my career, not bad for a self-taught picker (musician to proper folks). Some of my best-known folk songs and ballads include: "So Long It's Been Good to Know You" (1940), "This Land Is Your Land" (1956), "Hard Travelin'" (1959), "Pastures of Plenty" (1960), "Union Maid" (1961), and "Jesus Christ" (1961). I also recorded two albums of *Dust Bowl Ballads* (1964), with such songs as "Hard Road," "Do Re Mi," and "Reuben James." Earlier, I had gained success on the radio with my cousin Jack in a 15-minute radio show and with "Lefty Lou" Crissman in a regular Los Angeles radio program. In 1955, I was stricken with a serious nervous condition that led to my death on October 4, 1967, in New York City, New York.

My life began on July 14, 1912, in Okemah, Oklahoma. Both my parents had a great influence on my life; my father was a professional guitarist who sang Indian songs and blues, while my mother sang old songs and ballads. When I was about 13, I began making my own living by singing and playing the harmonica in saloons, halls, barber shops, migrant labor camps, hobo jungles, or wherever I could get people to listen. Through these experiences, I began writing ballads. But it was my uncle who got me on the right track, by teaching me to play the guitar and getting me a job with a dance band. His help led to jobs singing and playing at rodeos, country dances, and carnivals. Here I began taking old tunes and making up new words to them.

WHO AM I?

1. My life began on July 14, 1912, in Okemah, Oklahoma.

2. When I was 13, I began earning my own living by singing and playing the harmonica.
3. On the radio, I gained success with my cousin Jack and "Lefty Lou" Crissman.
4. I recorded two albums of *Dust Bowl Ballads* (1964).
5. Some of my best-known songs include: "So Long It's Been Good to Know You" (1940), "This Land Is Your Land" (1956), "Pastures of Plenty" (1960), and "Union Maid" (1961).

12

My scores for the films *The City* (1939), *Of Mice and Men* (1939), *Our Town* (1940), and *The Heiress* (1949, won an Academy Award in 1950) brought me international fame. I also gained enormous success with the ballet *Appalachian Spring* (1944), which won a New York Music Critics' Circle Award in 1945; its orchestral suite won a Pulitzer Prize in Music. The following year, I won another New York Music Critics' Circle Award for my *Third Symphony* (1946). My folk ballads in the ballets *Billy the Kid* (1938) and *Rodeo* (1942), and the patriotic ballad *A Lincoln Portrait* (1942), brought me earlier success. In 1964, I was honored with the Presidential Medal of Freedom.

I was born on November 14, 1900, in Brooklyn, New York. My early music training came from private piano teachers and a correspondence course which taught harmony. At the age of 15, I decided I wanted to be a composer. In 1917, I began taking harmony lessons from Rubin Goldmark. The following year, I graduated from high school and devoted the rest of my life to music. My first piano composition was "The Cat and the Mouse" (1918). In 1921, I became the first American to enroll in summer school at the Palace at Fontaineblea (Paris). I ended up staying three years, during which I wrote the compositions "Motets" and "Grohg." In 1924, I returned to the United States and a year later I produced my first substantial work, *Symphony with Organ* (1925).

WHO AM I?

1. I was born on November 14, 1900, in Brooklyn, New York.
2. At the age of 15, I decided I wanted to be a composer.

3. My first composition was "The Cat and the Mouse" (1918).
4. My folk ballads in the ballets *Billy the Kid* (1938) and *Rodeo* (1942), and the patriotic ballad *A Lincoln Portrait* (1942) were my early successes.
5. I gained international success with the film scores *The City* (1939), *Of Mice and Men* (1939), *Our Town* (1940), and *The Heiress* (1949).

Chapter Nine

Folk Heroes

<table><tr><td>

1

</td><td>

From the Allegheny River to the Saint Marys River, I planted tiny apple orchards in little patches of wilderness. With a leather sack filled with seeds that I brought from the cider presses of western Penn-sylvania, I traveled across virgin land planting my

</td></tr></table>

seeds. Often I would return to Pennsylvania to get more seeds; I made Ashland County, Ohio, my headquarters in 1810, because of its proximity to the west. I would travel hundreds of miles just to prune my orchards. It was during such a trip that I was stricken with pneumonia while repairing damages in a distant orchard. I appeared at the home of a settler in Allen County (in northeastern Indiana), where I laid down on his floor after din-ner and died on March 11, 1847.

I was born John Chapman on September 26, 1774, in Springfield, Massachusetts. As a child, I would wander off on long trips to explore the woods for birds and flowers. In 1797, I traveled to the Pennsylvania fron-tier, where I had already become a legendary folk hero. By 1801, I had arrived in the Ohio Territory around Steubenville, where I made my way across the virgin wilderness. Sometimes I would travel by horseback, sometimes by canoe, but mostly on foot (barefoot to be exact). You could always find me with my leather sack filled with apple seeds and my Bible. It was my mission in life to sow seeds and to perform missionary works for the Swedenborgianism religion. For my efforts, I was considered a Border saint by the pioneers and a medicine man by the Indians.

WHO AM I?

1. As a child, I would wander off on long trips to explore the woods for birds and flowers.

2. Sometimes I would travel by horseback, sometimes by canoe, but mostly on foot (barefoot to be exact).
3. I was considered a Border saint by the pioneers and a medicine man by the Indians.
4. I was born John Chapman on September 26, 1774, in Springfield, Massachusetts.
5. With a leather sack filled with apple seeds that I had brought from the cider presses of western Pennsylvania, I traveled across virgin land planting my seeds.

2 My former friend, Sheriff Patrick F. Garrett, launched a full-scale campaign to break up my 12-man gang in 1880. I was almost captured on Christmas Eve, 1880 in a gunfight at Fort Sumner, New Mexico, but was able to esape my captors. A few days later, I was finally captured along with three of my men. I was sentenced to death and placed in a prison in Lincoln County, New Mexico, for killing Sheriff James A. Brady. On April 28, 1881, I escaped from the prison (in the process killing two guards). Then on July 15, 1881, my life ended as I was trapped in a home in Fort Sumner and killed by Sheriff Pat Garrett's single gunshot. At the time of my death at the age of 21, I had killed 21 people in cold blood.

I was born William H. Bonney on November 23, 1859, in New York City, New York. At the age of 12, I began hanging out in saloons and gambling houses, where I became a skillful card player. I also committed my first murder that year, when I knifed a man for being rude to my mother. Four years later (near Fort Bowie, Arizona), my partner and I killed three nonviolent Indians for the furs off their backs. In 1877, I became a cowhand in New Mexico (Pecos Valley) and was credited with 12 murders. I accepted the leadership of the McSween faction in the Lincoln County, New Mexico, cattle war in February 1878, where I took part in many bloody skirmishes (one in which Sheriff James A. Brady and a deputy were killed).

WHO AM I?

1. At the age of 12, I began hanging out in saloons and gambling houses, where I became a skillful card player.

2. I also committed my first murder that year, when I knifed a man for being rude to my mother.
3. In 1877, I became a cowhand in New Mexico (Pecos Valley) and was credited with 12 murders.
4. I was born William H. Bonney on November 23, 1859, in New York City, New York.
5. My former friend, Sheriff Patrick F. Garrett, launched a full-scale campaign to break up my 12-man gang in 1880; on July 15, 1881, he ended my life with a single gunshot.

3 My prowess as a bear hunter, soldier, expert rifleman, and scout brought me legendary fame. As the story has been told, I once killed a 25 pound bear with my own hands and carried the bear home over my shoulders. In January 1836, I led a group of Tennessee volunteers to help Texas gain its independence from Mexico. The next month, we joined a group in San Antonio that were preparing to defend the Alamo against a powerful Mexican army. With a little more than 180 defenders we bravely fought to save the Alamo, but a bloody assault ensued on March 6, 1836, and all was lost. I fought to the bitter end for what I believed in. The state of Texas honored me by naming a city, county, and national forest after me.

I was born on August 17, 1786, in Greene City (Hawkins County), Tennessee. As a young man, I worked on a farm and rode cattle drives in Virginia. In 1806, I bought a farm of my own and began farming for myself. From 1813–1814, I served as an able scout in the Creek War under General Andrew Jackson. Three years after the war, I became a justice of the peace and a militia colonel in southwestern Tennessee. In 1821, I was elected to the Tennessee legislature. In 1827, I was finally elected to Congress as a Democrat, I was later reelected to a second term (1827–1831). After breaking with my party over a land bill, I became a Whig and returned to Congress in 1833. By 1835, I had lost my seat, which was fine with me (the Whigs had exploited me). I had had my fill of politics!

WHO AM I?

1. I was born on August 17, 1786, in Greene City, Tennessee.

2. From 1813–1814, I served as an able scout in the Creek War under General Andrew Jackson.
3. In 1821, I was elected to the Tennessee legislature.
4. With a little more than 180 defenders, we bravely fought to save the Alamo, but a bloody assault ensued on March 6, 1836, and all was lost.
5. I gained legendary fame for my prowess as a bear hunter (once killed a 25 pound bear with my own hands), soldier, expert rifleman, and scout.

4.

My brother Frank and I (along with a 12-member gang) became famous outlaws of the Old West. Our first bank robbery took place during broad daylight (the first such robbery in American history) in Liberty, Missouri, on February 13, 1866. Then after a bank robbery in Gallatin, Missouri, on December 17, 1869, my horse was left behind in the confusion and was identified as being mine, which put our names in all the local newspapers. In 1873, we began robbing trains, the first of which was the Rock Island train near Council Bluffs, Iowa. Here we dressed as Ku Klux Klansmen and loosened a rail in the tracks, which forced the train to stop; we netted $2,000 that day. On April 3, 1882, two of my men, Charles and Robert ("Bob") Ford were staying with my family, and while I was up on a chair straightening a picture, Bob Ford shot me in the back of the head for the reward money.

I was born to a Baptist minister on September 5, 1847, in Centerville (Clay County), Missouri. My good-natured sense of humor was often replaced by my quick, violent temper. It was during the Civil War skirmishes along the Kansas-Missouri border that my brother and I became involved with William Quantrill's irregulars. It soon became apparent that we had become involved with a group of men who sought criminal activities as a way of life. When we were not robbing banks and trains, my brother and I lived a quiet, normal life helping our mother out on her farm. In 1882, I settled down in St. Joseph, Missouri, with my wife and two children, under the assumed name of Thomas Howard, had joined the local Baptist church and completely turned my life around.

WHO AM I?

1. I was born on September 5, 1847, in Centerville, Missouri.
2. It was during the Civil War skirmishes along the Kansas-Missouri border that I became involved with William Quantrill.
3. In 1882, I settled down in St. Joseph, Missouri, under the assumed name of Thomas Howard.
4. My first bank robbery took place during broad daylight in Liberty, Missouri, on February 13, 1866.
5. With my brother Frank and a 12-member gang, I became a famous outlaw of the Old West.

| 5 | On March 17, 1775, 30 men and I laid out the Wilderness Road under Judge Richard Henderson's authority. It was here on the Kentucky River that we established a fort and settlement called Boonesborough. In February 1778, while gathering |

food for my party who were collecting salt at the Blue Licks, I was captured by the Shawnee Indians. Seventeen of us were adopted by the Shawnees; I became "Sheltowee" or "Big Turtle," the son of Chief Blackfish. I escaped on June 16, 1778, as I was being taken to Detroit to see the British governor. I traveled 160 miles in four days to warn the settlement of Boonesborough of the impending attack. We were able to defend ourselves against the attack and I later became a representative in the Kentucky legislature. I died on September 26, 1820, in St. Charles County, Missouri.

I was born on November 2, 1734, near Reading, Pennsylvania. As a young boy, I became interested in hunting and trapping under the watchful eye of my father. At the age of 12, I used the rifle he had given me earlier to hunt game and furs. On our farm I helped my father with the farming, weaving, and blacksmithing until 1755, when I joined General Edward Braddock on his expedition to Fort Duquesne as a blacksmith/teamster. In 1769, five others and I traveled through the Cumberland Gap to Kentucky to establish a base at Station Camp Creek. After two years, I returned to North Carolina to pack up my family and move them to Kentucky (Clinch River area).

WHO AM I?

1. I was born on November 2, 1734, near Reading, Pennsylvania.
2. On our farm I helped my father with the farming, weaving, and blacksmithing until 1755, when I joined General Edward Braddock on his expedition to Fort Duquesne.
3. In February 1778, I was captured by the Shawnee Indians who adopted me and named me "Sheltowee" or "Big Turtle."
4. Five others and I traveled through the Cumberland Gap to Kentucky to establish a base at Station Camp Creek in 1769.
5. On March 17, 1775, 30 men and I laid out the Wilderness Road and established a settlement called Boonesborough.

In May 1875, I joined the Newton-Jenney geological expedition dressed in manly attire. We left Fort Laramie under the protection of 400 soldiers, traveling through hostile Indian territory to the Black Hills. Soon I became General George Crock's camp follower, but an officer booted me out of the regiment when he discovered that I was a woman. The following year in Deadwood Gulch, South Dakota, I met Wild Bill Hickok during the gold-mining boom. It was rumored that we were sweethearts, but Bill was always devoted to his wife and children. In 1878, I cared for victims of a smallpox epidemic in Deadwood. After my work was completed I resumed my wandering, selling a leaflet about my life story as a Pony Express rider and scout for General Custer. My wanderings ended on August 1, 1903, in Terry, South Dakota.

I was born Martha Jane Cannary around May 1, 1852 in Princeton, Missouri. By the age of 15, both my parents had died, leaving me to roam the West on my own. Dressed in manly attire (a buckskin suit and wide-brimmed hat), I began going to saloons and dance halls in Montana, drinking and swearing with the best of them. In the early 1870s, I moved to Wyoming to seek out new adventures. On September 25, 1891, I married Clinton Burke in El Paso, Texas. He could not handle me, so he up and left one day.

WHO AM I?

1. In 1878, I cared for the victims of a smallpox epidemic in Deadwood Gulch, South Dakota.
2. On September 25, 1891, I married Clinton Burke in El Paso, Texas. He could not handle me, so he up and left one day.
3. Dressed in manly attire (a buckskin suit and wide-brimmed hat), I began going to saloons and dance halls in Montana, drinking and swearing with the best of them.
4. In 1876 (Deadwood Gulch, South Dakota), I met Wild Bill Hickok; it was rumored that we were sweethearts, but Bill was always devoted to his wife and children.
5. I was born Martha Jane Cannary around May 1, 1852, in Princeton, Missouri.

7

American folklore tells of a railway workman who went up against an automatic steam-powered drill, a very powerful drill. One day a salesman came by with his drill, and he bet the captain of our crew that his drill could outperform any man. The captain took him up on the bet, pitting me against the machine. That day I drove the steel bits into the rocks with a powerful 200-pound force. The machine started drilling, setting an enormous pace. I picked up the pace, using my strength and skill. The battle raged on until I finally emerged as the winner. But the strain was just too much; I collapsed and died of exhaustion. Since then I have been honored with an American folk song that remains popular today.

It is said that my story is based on a man in West Virginia who died in a cave-in while blasting the Big Bend Tunnel for the Chesapeake and Ohio Railroad in the early 1870s. Others say it was in Alabama in 1882. This man was a powerful man who excelled at driving steel bits into granite rocks. He could work shifts of ten hours straight, outlasting every man on his crew. That is why he was chosen to be at the head of the line, driving his cold steel into the hard rocks. A folk legend was born.

WHO AM I?

1. I could drive steel bits into rocks with a powerful 200-pound force.
2. It is said that my story is based on a man in West Virginia who died in a cave-in while blasting the Big Bend Tunnel for the Chesapeake and Ohio Railroad in the early 1870s.
3. One day a salesman came by with his drill, and he bet the captain of our crew that his drill could out perform any man.
4. I finally emerged as the winner, but the strain was just too much; I collapsed and died of exhaustion.
5. American folklore tells of a railway workman who went up against an automatic steam-powered drill and won; the story is captured in a popular folk song.

8   My marksmanship with a rifle and shotgun brought me international fame; it also brought me a husband. I met my future husband, Frank E. Butler (a successful marksman and vaudeville actor in his own right), at a Cincinnati shooting match. That day I beat him by one point, but some years later we were married and he became my manager and assistant on our circus tours; in the end we both won. By 1885, we had signed on with Buffalo Bill's Wild West show that was on tour in Louisville at the time. Earlier, he had seen us in New Orleans on tour with the Sells Brothers Circus. He liked what he saw and invited us to join his show. For the next 17 years, I served as the show's star attraction. I delighted audiences with my skillful feats, such as shooting a dime in mid-air, shooting a playing card full of holes at 30 paces, shooting a cigarette from my husband's lips, and shooting 943 glass balls out of 1,000 with a .22 rifle.

I was born Phoebe Anne on August 13, 1860, in Patterson Township (Drake County), Ohio. At the age of nine, I helped support the family by shooting rabbits and quails that I later sold at market. My prowess with a rifle was so great that within five years I was able to pay off the mortgage on our farm. My fame as a marksman continued throughout my life. I did not even let a train accident in 1901 (which left me partially paralyzed) stop me. For the next 20 years, I set record after record. After a five-year retirement, I died on November 2, 1926, in Greenville, Ohio.

WHO AM I?

1. I was born on August 13, 1860, in Patterson Township, Ohio.
2. My prowess with a rifle was so great that within five years I was able to pay off the mortage on our farm.
3. I met my future husband, Frank E. Butler, (a successful marksman and vaudeville actor in his own right), at a Cincinnati shooting match, which I won by one point.
4. By 1885, we had signed on with Buffalo Bill's Wild West Show, where I delighted audiences with my skillful shooting feats.
5. The musical *Annie Get Your Gun* (1946) is based on my life.

9 A famous railroad ballad tells of my plight as an Illinois Central Railroad engineer who dies in a collision while trying to make up time to keep his Chicago to New Orleans run on schedule. The fateful night was April 30, 1900, a foul weather day with lots of fog and thick clouds. That night I took old 382 (thought to be the "Cannonball Express") out of Central Station 90 minutes late. To make up the time, I kept the fire stoked to the maximum. As I raced down the tracks near Vaughan, Mississippi, another freight was headed northbound (I was headed southbound) on the same tracks. Unable to stop in time, our engine collided with the other train's caboose and two other cars at 3:52 (only two minutes overdue at Vaughan). When they checked through the wreckage, they found me dead behind the wheel.

I was born John Luther on May 14, 1864, in Cayce, Kentucky. My nickname came from my childhood home of Cayce, Kentucky. An early interest in trains led to a job as an engineer on the Illinois Central Railroad. I was well-respected by my fellow workers, who enjoyed working under me. The original ballad of my story was told by Wallace Saunders, my engine wiper on that fateful trip. By 1909, T.L. Seibert and E.W. Newton had revised the ballad for the vaudeville stage. Several versions followed, and it was added to our American folklore. In 1938, Robert Ardrey wrote a play in my honor.

WHO AM I?

1. I was born on May 14, 1864, in Cayce, Kentucky.
2. An early interest in trains led to a job as an engineer on the Illinois Central Railroad.
3. On April 30, 1900, I took old 382 out of Central Station 90 minutes late.
4. My nickname came from my childhood home of Cayce, Kentucky.
5. A famous railroad ballad tells of my plight as a Illinois Central Railroad engineer who dies in a collision while trying to make up time to keep my Chicago to New Orleans run on schedule.

My Southern tales about animals who take on human qualities were first told by me to my master's little boy. The tales told of the adventures of Brer Rabbit and his other animal friends. These stories included: "Brer Rabbit's Frolic," "Brer Rabbit Treats the Creeturs to a Race," and "Brer Rabbit and the Gold Mine." Brer Rabbit's other friends included Brer Fox (e.g., "Brer Rabbit Causes Brer Fox to Lose His Hide" and "The Story of Brer Fox and Little Mr. Cricket"), Brer B'ar (e.g., "How Brer Rabbit Saved Brer B'ar's Life"), Brer Wolf and others. These stories were later collected and retold by Joel Chandler Harris.

There is not much known about my life, except that I served as a kindly house servant on a plantation in the South. To entertain my master's children, especially his little boy, I would tell tales of Brer Rabbit and his friends. These include: "Brother Bear's Big House," "How Mr. Lion Lost His Wool," "Why Mr. Possum Loves Peace," "How Mr. Rooster Lost His Dinner," and "Why the Alligator's Back Is Rough," among many others. These humorous stories were always told in the black dialect of the South. The tales have since become masterpieces of American folklore.

WHO AM I?

1. Little is known about my life, except that I served as a kindly house servant on a plantation in the South.
2. My Southern tales about animals who take on human qualities were first told by me to my master's little boy.
3. Some of these stories were about "Brother Bear's Big House," "How Mr. Lion Lost His Wool," "Why Mr. Possum Loves Peace," and "How Mr. Rooster Lost His Dinner."
4. These stories were later collected and retold by Joel Chandler Harris.
5. These humorous stories told of the adventures of Brer Rabbit and his other animal friends and were told in the black dialect of the South.

11

I was raised by coyotes who found me lost in the desert as an infant. As I grew, my attentions turned toward being an outlaw, Indian fighter, and cowboy. Legend has it that I invented the lasso and the six-shooter and taught my fellow cowboys how to rope, brand cattle, and ride bucking broncos. It is also said that I single-handedly dug the Rio Grande. Once I even rode bareback on an Oklahoma cyclone on a bet from a fellow cowboy. My hobbies included taming mountain lions and wrestling bears. It was a good life, full of adventure, until one day I drank whiskey laced with barbed wire and fish hooks, which ended my days of fun and frolic.

The legend of my life as a cowboy hero of the American Southwest began in 1923 with the publication of a story written by Edward O'Reilly. He told the story of a man who was bigger than life, with adventures to match. One such adventure happened on the New Mexico line, when I ran into a 12-foot rattlesnake. Being a sportin' man, I let the rattlesnake bite me three times. When all was said and done, I wrapped the rattlesnake about my neck and continued on the line. As I walked through a canyon, a large mountain lion jumped on my back. It was a fierce fight, with fur flying everywhere. When it was all over, I had the mountain lion lickin' my face. So I threw my saddle and bridle on him, jumped on his back, and rode across the mountains with the rattlesnake still wrapped around my neck.

WHO AM I?

1. I was raised by coyotes who found me lost in the desert as an infant.
2. As I grew, my attentions turned toward being an outlaw, Indian fighter, and cowboy.
3. A cowboy hero from the American Southwest, I was bigger than life, with adventures to match.
4. Legend has it that I invented the lasso and the six-shooter. It is even said that I single-handedly dug the Rio Grande.
5. Once I even rode bareback on an Oklahoma cyclone on a bet from a fellow cowboy.

12

I was a favorite legendary hero of the frontier lumber camps. The stories were exaggerations, but they were always told in all truthfulness. Once I worked up 40 acres of timber into 246 million feet of lumber. Then there was the time I got in a fight with my foreman over how a job should be done. We began throwing pieces of a mountain at each other and eventually formed the Black Hills in South Dakota. I also had a hand in the formation of the Mississippi River. My ox Babe (measured 42 axhandles between the eyes) was pulling a tank of water on a sled down from Lake Superior. The tank got a hole in it, and the water ran down the hill to form the Mississippi.

When I was just three weeks old, I rocked my cradle so hard that I leveled four square miles of trees. As I jumped out of my cradle for the first time, I started a 70-foot tidal wave in the Bay of Fundy. While playing in the backyard, I dug Puget Sound. When the job was done, I hung my Big Dipper in the sky close to the Milky Way. In the late 1800s, stories like these were told in lumber camps from the Great Lakes to the Pacific Northwest. By 1914, these stories had been collected into booklets by W.B. Laughead, a Minnesota advertising man who worked to promote the Red River Lumber Company.

WHO AM I?

1. When I was just three weeks old, I rocked my cradle so hard that I leveled four square miles of trees.
2. As I jumped out of my cradle for the first time, I started a 70-foot tidal wave in the Bay of Fundy.
3. Then there was the time I got in a fight with my foreman over how a job should be done. We began throwing pieces of a mountain at each other and eventually formed the Black Hills.
4. Once I worked up 40 acres of timber into 246 million feet of lumber.
5. My ox Babe (42 axhandles between the eyes) was pulling a tank of water on a sled down from Lake Superior. The tank got a hole in it, and the water ran down the hill to form the Mississippi River.

Chapter Ten
Merchants/Entrepreneurs

1

My business was based on the "Golden Rule" and "Penney Principles." Today, it is one of the world's largest retail department store chains. It all began in 1902, when T.M. Callahan offered me the opportunity to buy a one-third partnership with Johnston's and Callahan's. That same year (just selling dry goods, weaving apparel, and shoes) sales totaled $29,000 at the Kemmerer, Wyoming store. By 1911, my chain had grown to 22 stores.

Fourteen years later, I teamed up with Ralph W. Gwinn to form the J.C.P.–Gwinn Corporation, which established Penney Farms (a Florida Scientific Farming community). By 1927, my chain of stores were fully incorporated (original incorporation was January 16, 1913), and later the headquarters were moved to New York. I opened my 500th store in Hamilton, Missouri (my hometown) in 1924. By 1946, sales had reached $676,584,135. At the time of my death on February 12, 1971, my chain had grown to 1,660 stores.

I was born on September 16, 1875, in Hamilton, Missouri. When I was just eight years old, my father found me a job with a local merchant. He thought it was time for me to start earning my own way. After high school (Hamilton High), on February 4, 1895, I began working as a clerk in a dry goods store (William M. Hall & Company) in Hamilton.

Two years later, I suffered from health problems and had to move to Colorado. Here I worked briefly as a clerk for a Denver department store. Then I tried my hand at a meat and bakery business that proved unsuccessful. This led to a position with T.M. Callahan (1879) for $50 a month at his Evanston, Wyoming, store. The rest, you could say, is history!

WHO AM I?

1. I was born on September 16, 1875, in Hamilton, Missouri.
2. When I was just eight years old, my father found me a job with a local merchant.
3. At the time of my death on February 12, 1971, my retail chain had grown to 1,660 stores.
4. My business was based on the "Golden Rule" and the "Penney Principles."
5. In 1925, I teamed up with Ralph W. Gwinn to form the J.C.P.–Gwinn Corporation, which established Penney Farms.

| 2 |

In 1954, while working as a "multi-mixer" distributor, I came upon a small San Bernardino, California restaurant owned by Mac and Dick McDonald, who were doing a wonderful business selling just 15-cent hamburgers, French fries, and milk shakes. A year later, I began incorporating their assembly line methods into a drive-in restaurant franchise (the brothers received one-half of one percent royalty on the gross receipts). On April 15, 1955, I opened my first drive-in restaurant in Des Plaines, Illinois. By 1960, there were 228 franchises with $37 million in annual sales. The following year, I bought out the McDonald brothers for $2.7 million. My 2,000th restaurant was opened in 1972, with sales over $1 billion and 10 billion hamburgers sold. I also established "Hamburger University" in Elk Grove, Illinois, that offers a 19-day intensive training program for owner/operators to learn the ins and outs of the franchise business. At the completion of the course, a "Bachelor of Hamburgerology" is awarded. I died on January 24, 1984, in San Diego, California.

I was born on October 5, 1902, in Chicago, Illinois. At an early age, I vowed that I would not have to struggle to make a living like my father. In my sophomore year of high school (15 years old), I left to become an ambulance driver (World War I) in the Red Cross Ambulance Corps. After the war I returned to my hometown and became a jazz pianist (my mother taught me to play the piano at the age of six) with various bands and orchestras. Dissatisfied with the long hours of a musician, I went to work for the Lily-Tulip Cup Company as a paper cup salesman. Seeking a new challenge and more money, I went to work for the radio station WGES

(Chicago) as their musical director. Here I discovered a song-and-dance team called "Sam and Henry" (later known as "Amos 'n' Andy"). After just a year and half, I resigned to sell real estate (Florida) during the 1920s' land boom. The boom went bust in 1926 and I returned to playing the piano in nightclubs. But the pay was lousy, so I returned to the Lily-Tulip Cup Company as their Midwest sales manager.

WHO AM I?

1. I was born on October 5, 1902, in Chicago, Illinois.
2. In my sophomore year of high school, I left to become an ambulance driver in the Red Cross Ambulance Corps.
3. I worked as a paper cup salesman and Midwest sales manager for the Lily-Tulip Cup Company.
4. I established "Hamburger University," which awards a "Bachelor of Hamburgerology" for completing the 19-day program.
5. In 1954, while working as a "multi-mixer" distributor, I came upon a small San Bernardino restaurant owned by Mac and Dick McDonald.

3 My success began under the employ of W.H. Moore in Watertown, New York (1877). That same year, I talked Mr. Moore into selling all the items in his store for 5-cents a piece; I had heard about a store that had done this. The idea proved successful, and Mr. Moore set me up in a 5-cent store of my own in Utica, New York, which failed in only three months. Mr. Moore did not give up on me; he set me up in another store in Lancaster, Pennsylvania (1879), with a 5- and 10-cent theme. The venture proved very successful, so I began opening other stores in other cities. By 1912, I had established a chain of stores that still bears my name today. Seven years later, my chain had grown to more than 1,000 stores in the United States and Canada. After amassing a tremendous fortune I built a 60-story (800 feet) building which bears my name in New York (designed by Cass Gilbert); it was the world's tallest building at the time. At the time of my death on August 8, 1919, sales had reached more than $100 million; I had a personal fortune of $65 million.

I was born on April 13, 1852, in Rodman, New York. My early years were spent attending one-room schoolhouses (Greatbend, New York) and playing storekeeper (my favorite game). In my teens, I fulfilled my dream of a mercantile career by attending a business school (two terms) in Watertown and clerking in a village grocery store when I was 19 years old to gain experience (no pay). After two years I left to clerk at a store in Watertown for a six-month trial period (received $3.50 a week after working three months without pay). In 1875, I was employed by a Watertown man who established a store (based on a 99-cent store in Watertown) in Port Huron, Michigan. I was such a poor salesman that my boss cut my salary from $10.00 a week to $8.50. The stress of my failure took a heavy toll on my health, so I returned to my father's farm to regain my strength.

WHO AM I?

1. I was born on April 13, 1852, in Rodman, New York.
2. My favorite game as a child was playing store.
3. In 1875, I was employed by a Watertown man who established a store (based on a 99-cent store) in Port Huron, Michigan.
4. I talked W.H. Moore into selling all the items in his store for 5-cents a piece.
5. With the success of my first 5- and 10-cent store, I established a chain of stores "worth" looking up.

My restaurant business had its humble beginnings in 1929, when I opened a gas station (Corbin, Kentucky) that also served food to hungry travelers. My Southern-style cooking (especially my mother's pan-fried chicken) caught on. I closed the gas station and opened the Sanders' Cafe to meet the demand. By 1939, with the invention of the pressure cooker, I had developed a moisture-packed chicken with a blend of 11 herbs and spices that is still "finger lickin' good" today. In 1956 (at the age of 65), I took to the road in my 1946 Ford to establish a chicken franchise business. I was only able to get five franchises in the first two years to cook their chicken my way. By 1960, the number had risen to 200. In 1964, with more than 600 franchises, I sold the business to John Y. Brown, Jr., for $2 million. I died on December 16, 1980, near Shelbyville, Kentucky.

I was born on September 9, 1890, near Henryville, Indiana. Upon my father's death when I was six, I was forced to learn to cook. By the following year, I had become proficient at breads, vegetables, and meats. At the beginning of 7th grade (12 years old), I left school to become a farmhand on a farm near Greenwood, Indiana. When I was 15, I left farming (which I did not care for) for the next 25 years to pursue low paying odd jobs (e.g., streetcar conductor, buggy painter, insurance salesman, ferryboat operator, and soldier). After taking a correspondence course in law and earning a Doctor of Law degree from Southern University, I began practicing law in the Justice of the Peace courts in Little Rock, Arkansas. Soon tiring of law, my attentions turned back to cooking. I took an eight-week course in Restaurant and Hotel Management at Cornell University, which put me on the road to franchise history.

WHO AM I?

1. My life began on September 9, 1890, near Henryville, Indiana.
2. By the time I was seven, I had become proficient at breads, vegetables, and meats.
3. My Southern-style cooking (especially my mother's pan-fried chicken) caught on in Corbin, Kentucky.
4. After selling the company in 1964, I remained on as their spokesperson dressed in my white, Southern gentleman's suit.
5. In 1939, I developed chicken with a blend of 11 herbs and spices that is still "finger lickin' good" today.

5 In 1889, I retired from my mail order watch business (sold it for $100,000) and moved to Iowa to become a banker. But I found the work boring and returned to the mail order business. Prevented under a contract from returning to the business in Chicago for three years, I established my mail order business in Minneapolis. Here I rehired my watchmaker, Alvah Curtis Roebuck, and began the A.C. Roebuck & Company (later added my name to the company; today Roebuck has been dropped). In 1893, we moved the headquarters to Chicago, where it became very successful. Our catalog grew from 25 items of watches and jewelry to 1,000 pages, within just a few years. Two years later, Roebuck sold his interest to Julius Rosenwald, a Chicago clothing manufacturer. Our sales at this time were $500,000; within five years, sales reached $11 million. I remained as president of the company until my retirement in 1909. Even after my death on September 28, 1914, in Waukesha, Wisconsin, my company remains one of the largest retail department stores, with a thriving mail order catalog business.

I was born on December 7, 1863, in Stewartville, Minnesota. To support my mother and sisters after my father's death when I was 17 years old, I went to work for the Minneapolis & St. Louis Railway. Later, I began moonlighting by selling coal, lumber, and various commodities purchased by the Indians. In 1886, when a local jeweler refused to take shipment of a load of watches, I advertised the watches at bargain prices. The watches sold quickly, giving me an idea for a new money-making business. In a few months, I left my railroad job to establish my own mail order business in Minneapolis, which I later moved to Chicago.

WHO AM I?

1. I was born on December 7, 1863, in Stewartville, Minnesota.
2. To support my mother and sisters after my father's death, I went to work for the Minneapolis & St. Louis Railway.
3. In 1886, I began my career selling watches in the mail order business.
4. My catalog grew from 25 items of watches and jewelry to 1,000 pages of various other items.
5. I hired Alvah Curtis Roebuck (a watchmaker) to make adjustments and repairs on the watches that I had sold.

With $5,000 out of my own pocket, I created a multi-million dollar cosmetic empire (which bears my name) that is almost exclusively staffed by women. My company's sales incentive program includes cream-colored Oldsmobiles, pink Cadillacs, and gold, diamond-studded bumblebees as symbols of success. The sales staff is composed of wives and mothers who set their own hours to fit their families' schedules. These V.I.P.s ("Very Important Performers") make up a personal network of door-to-door salesperformers. We beat our competitors with lower prices and a streamlined product line of 45 items that stresses skin care. It all began on September 13, 1963, when I opened my first store in a Dallas office complex, with a single inventory of skin creams. It still remains the base of my product line today.

I was born on (a lady never gives her birth date); let's just say I was a World War I baby in Hot Wels, Texas. My rough childhood (at the age of seven, I cared for my father who had tuberculosis, while my mother worked) would prepare me for the struggle ahead. When I was just 17, I married a local boy who left me after eight years of marriage with three small children to raise on my own. To support my family, I began selling Stanley Home Products door-to-door while my children were in school. Then I went to work for the World Gift Company, which made me a better offer and whose company I helped to expand across the United States. Finding that a woman could not be promoted to the executive suite, I resigned in 1963 and later started my own business.

WHO AM I?

1. I was born on (a lady never gives her birth date); let's just say I was a World War I baby in Hot Wels, Texas.
2. At the age of seven, I cared for my father, who had tuberculosis, while my mother worked to support the family.
3. My door-to-door salesperformers offer a product line of 45 items that stresses skin care.
4. On September 13, 1963, I opened my first store in Dallas with a single inventory of skin creams.
5. My company's sales incentive program includes cream-colored Oldsmobiles, pink Cadillacs, and gold, diamond-studded bumblebees as symbols of success.

7

Our trademark of 31 different ice cream flavors (a different flavor for each day of the month) has included such exotic flavors as: Plum Nuts (plums, vanilla, and walnuts), Cha Cha Cha (cherry chocolate chip), and Tanganilla (tangerine/vanilla). By 1983, there were over 500 flavors, including the classics Jamoca Almond Fudge and Fudge Brownie. Over the years we have continually rotated the flavors to keep them exciting to our regulars; now these flavors include a selection of sugar free ice creams and yogurts. The whole concept began in 1947, when we became partners. The following year, we had eight stores and a plan for a franchise. By 1960, we had over 100 stores. When we sold the franchise business in 1967 for about $12 million, we had a total of 500 stores (it reached over 2,000 stores in 1978 when Robbins retired).

I was born in 1913 in Chicago, Illinois. My interest in ice cream began surfacing in World War II as a navy PX operator. Stationed in the New Hebrides, I started churning out tasty ice cream flavors, using the island's tropical fruits. My brother-in-law and partner's interest in ice cream began at his father's dairy farm, where he learned ice cream making and began experimenting with different flavor combinations. Our interests took us in different directions; I opened my own shop in Pasadena (Burton's Ice Cream) and he opened a shop in Glendale (Snowbird Ice Cream Store). But in the end our love of ice cream brought us together.

WHO AM I?

1. I was born in 1913 in Chicago, Illinois, and later became a transplanted Californian.
2. My interest in ice cream began during World War II as a PX operator.
3. I opened my own shop in Pasadena (Burton's Ice Cream) and my future partner opened a shop in Glendale (Snowbird Ice Cream Store).
4. By 1983, there were over 500 ice cream flavors, including the classics Jamoca Almond Fudge and Fudge Brownie.
5. Our trademark is 31 different ice cream flavors: a different flavor for each day of the month.

8

My idea of buying in large quantities (for cash) from the manufacturer and selling directly to the farmer (for cash) at discount prices, revolutionized the retail department store business. By 1872, with the $1,600 I had saved up (the Chicago fire of 1871 had taken the rest of my savings) and the $800 from my partner George R. Thorne, we began our store in a livery stable loft. With our limited selection of dry-goods and a one-page catalog, we offered our customers affordable, discount prices with a liberal return policy. Our catalog grew to 150 pages in 1876, and our annual sales increased to $1 million in 1888. By the time of my death on December 7, 1913, in Highland Park, Illinois, annual sales had reached $40 million. Today, the retail department store that bears my name still satisfies customers with Extra Values and Chairman's Choices.

I was born on February 17, 1843, in Chatham, New Jersey. I left school at the age of 14 to become a trade apprentice, which I soon left to pursue work in a barrel-stave factory. To earn more money, I later worked in a brickyard as a day laborer. At the age of 19, I took my first step toward retail success as a clerk in a St. Joseph, Michigan, general store. My hard work paid off, and within three years I became the store's manager (salary increased from $5 to $100-a-month). In 1865, I left to take a position with Field, Palmer & Leiter (a larger store in Chicago). After two years I left to join Willis, Gregg & Brown (a wholesale dry-goods house), which soon went bankrupt.

WHO AM I?

1. I was born on February 17, 1843, in Chatham, New Jersey.
2. At the age of 19, I took my first step toward retail success as a clerk in a St. Joseph, Michigan, general store.
3. In 1872, with the $1,600 that I had saved up and the $800 from my partner, we began our store in a livery stable loft.
4. We offered a one-page catalog that grew to 150 pages in 1876 and which is no longer in use today.
5. Today, the retail department store that bears my name still satisfies customers with Extra Values and Chairman's Choices.

My homemade chocolate chip cookies (taken from my Aunt Della's own recipe) have become "famous" from coast to coast. With the help of B.J. Gilmore and other famous investors, I was able to open my very first store (March 10, 1975) on Sunset Boulevard in Hollywood, California. The sign out front read: "THE ORIGINAL HOME OF THE FAMOUS _____ CHOCOLATE CHIP COOKIE." The day before I had handed out samples on the street to introduce my cookie to the community. It worked! Today, the company enjoys a successful wholesale business, selling cookies to Macy's (formerly Bloomingdale's), chic boutiques, and various grocery stores nationwide. There is even a bakery on the East Coast. Not bad for a former shoeshine boy from Tallahassee.

I was born on July 1, 1936, in Tallahassee, Florida. My interest in business began at an early age, when I set up my own successful shoeshine business (I was known for my professional shoeshines). Then I expanded my business opportunities by delivering newspapers, first for the Tallahassee *Democrat*, then for several New York newspapers (moved there when I was 12). When I reached high school (Food Trades Vocational High School), my attentions turned to cooking and a job at the Essex House Hotel as a pantry worker. After serving in the United States Air Force (signed up when I was 17), I enrolled at the Collegiate Secretarial Institute and found work as a store clerk at Saks Fifth Avenue; it was here that I learned the most about business. This led to the William Morris Agency (seven years) and work as a personal manager/promoter for rock and roll groups (seven years).

WHO AM I?

1. I was born on July 1, 1936, in Tallahassee, Florida.
2. My interest in business began at an early age when I set up my own successful shoeshine business.
3. When I reached high school, my attentions turned to cooking and a job at the Essex House Hotel as a pantry worker.
4. I learned the ins-and-outs of business as a store clerk for Saks Fifth Avenue.
5. My homemade chocolate chip cookies (taken from my Aunt Della's own recipe) have become "famous" from coast to coast.

10 Today, my stores are known by the big "K," which represents everyday low prices and blue light specials. It all began in 1899, when I traded my half-ownership in a 5-and-10 store in Memphis for my partner's half-ownership in our Detroit store to become sole proprietor of the store. The 5-and-10 idea soon caught on and I began opening stores throughout the country. By 1907, I was operating six stores under the family name. Five years later, I incorporated the business with 85 stores and a capital of $7 million. At the time of my retirement in 1925, there were 930 merchandise stores with a capital of $100 million. I died on October 18, 1966, in East Stroudsburg, Pennsylvania.

I was born on July 31, 1867, in Bald Mount (Lackawanna County), Pennsylvania. After attending Fairview Academy I went on to the Eastman Business College (Poughkeepsie, New York). In 1886, I taught school at the Gower's School (Monroe County, Pennsylvania), but soon left to seek a career in business. My first job in the business area was with Patrick Ward (a grocery store owner in Scranton, Pennsylvania), as a clerk and delivery man. From 1889–1892, I worked as a bookkeeper in a hardware store and later worked as a traveling salesman, selling hardware and tinware (1892–1897). My biggest break came when I joined John G. McCror (as a part owner and assistant buyer) in opening two 5-and-10 stores.

WHO AM I?

1. I was born on July 31, 1867, in Bald Mount, Pennsylvania.
2. After attending Fairview Academy I went on to the Eastman Business College.
3. My first job in the business arena was with Patrick Ward as a clerk and delivery man.
4. At the time of my retirement in 1925, there were 930 merchandise stores with a capital of $100 million.
5. Today, my stores are known by the big "K," which represents everyday low prices and blue light specials.

11

My Wal-Mart enterprise began in 1948, with the purchase of my first Ben Franklin 5- and 10-cent store in Newport, Arkansas. Sales reached $225,000 that first year, which prompted me to buy other Ben Franklin franchises. By 1968, I had 24 stores (four states) with annual sales of $12.5 million; Class A stores were doing $400,000 a year and over, Class B were doing $200,000, and my Class C stores were doing $100,000. My idea of building large variety stores in small towns was meeting with great success. By the 1990s, I had 1,500 stores (22 states) with annual sales of $26 billion. With the success of my chain of variety stores, I opened Sam's Wholesale Club (first one was in Oklahoma City, April 1983). By the end of the year, I had three clubs with annual sales of $37 million. Those numbers increased to 105 clubs, with sales of $5 billion, in the early 1990s.

I was born on March 29, 1918, in Kingfisher, Oklahoma. My high school years were filled with activities. Not only was I a good student, but I also became an Eagle Scout, bottled and sold excess milk from my father's cow (my first big business venture), served as junior class vice president, senior student body president, played football and basketball, worked various odd jobs (delivering newspapers and working as a clerk in the 5- and 10-cent store), and joined every club and organization my high school offered. This also carried over into college (University of Missouri), where I sold newspapers and was a waiter, lifeguard, and R.O.T.C. cadet. After graduating in 1940 with a degree in business administration (economics major), I received my commission in the United States Army reserves.

WHO AM I?

1. I was born on March 29, 1918, in Kingfisher, Oklahoma.
2. While in high school, I became an Eagle Scout and served as senior student body president.
3. In 1948, I bought my first Ben Franklin 5- and 10-cent store in Newport, Arkansas.
4. I opened my first Sam's Wholesale Club in Oklahoma City; now I have 105 clubs, with sales of $5 billion.
5. By the 1990s, I had built my Wal-Mart enterprise into 1,500 stores, with annual sales of $26 billion.

12

Chocolate chip cookies have been my speciality since I was 13, but I never thought about turning them into a profit-making business until I started baking them for my husband's clients, who just loved them. Over the years, I had perfected a recipe using the finest ingredients. I opened my first store, "The Chocolate Chippery," in Palo Alto at Liddicoat's grocery. Then I opened "Debbi's Chocolate Chippery" on August 18, 1977, at The Stanford Barn, selling 3-inch round, half-inch thick cookies for 25-cents each. I began adding more stores and incorporated my business in 1979. My chocolate chip cookies were such a success that I began adding other cookies (e.g., Peanut Butter Dreams and Pecan Whites), brownies (e.g., pecan fudge), ice cream (butter pecan), candy (Macadamia Royals), muffins (e.g., strawberry bran), and gift items. By 1986, sales had reached $87 million.

My life began on September 18, 1956, in Oakland, California. My future business success began while still in junior high school, when I worked for the Oakland A's as their third-base ball girl. When I was 15, I found work at the local Mervyn's Department Store (boy's department). Here I taught myself organization and customer service techniques. I left when I was 17, to become a water-skier at Marine World. After graduating from Alameda High (at 17), I packed up and moved to Lake Tahoe, where I found work as a governess. I lasted just a few months; five kids were just too much for me. So I returned home to work part-time in retail until my marriage at 18.

WHO AM I?

1. My life began on September 18, 1956, in Oakland, California.
2. At 13, I was the Oakland A's third-base ball girl.
3. I started baking chocolate chip cookies when I was 13.
4. Today, my stores offer Peanut Butter Dreams, Pecan Whites, Oatmeal Raisin Nut, White Chunk's with macadamia nuts, and lots more.
5. My business went from "The Chocolate Chippery" to "Debbi's Chocolate Chippery"; now it goes by my married name.

Chapter Eleven
Artists

1

My *Saturday Evening Post* covers made me famous throughout the world. The covers depicted small town, everyday living in realistic, humorous tones. My first cover for the magazine appeared in May 1916; they continued at a rate of ten covers a year. The covers include: "No Swimming" (June 4, 1921), "Saying Grace" (November 24, 1951), "Walking to Church" (April 4, 1953), and "Girl at the Mirror" (March 6, 1954). My other works include: illustations for Mark Twain's two books *The Adventures of Tom Sawyer* and *The Adventures of Huckleberry Finn*, the mural in the Nassau Tavern (Princeton, New Jersey) called the "Four Freedoms," an oil sketch from that mural called "Freedom of Speech," and various other covers and illustrations for well-known periodicals. I made my final brush stroke on November 8, 1978, in Stockbridge, Massachusetts.

I was born on February 3, 1894, in New York City, New York. My father was an amateur painter and my grandfather was an English portrait painter; both were very influential throughout my early life. At the age of 13, I took art lessons at the Chase School of Art, where I pursued my love of drawing. Later, I attended the National Academy of Design, and at 16, I left high school to enroll in the Art Student's League (won two scholarships). Here I was nicknamed "The Dream" and opened my first studio with a classmate. When I was 17, I painted illustrations for McBride & Nast publications. These include: a children's book, *Tell-Me-Why Stories*, a historical work on Champlain, and a camping volume in *Boy's Life*.

WHO AM I?

1. I was born on February 3, 1894, in New York City, New York.

2. At the age of 16, I won two scholarships to the Art Student's League. Here I was nicknamed "The Dream."
3. A year later, I illustrated the children's book, *Tell-Me-Why Stories.*
4. Later, I illustrated Mark Twain's two books *The Adventures of Tom Sawyer* and *The Adventures of Huckleberry Finn.*
5. My *Saturday Evening Post* covers depicted small town, everyday life in realistic, humorous tones.

2

At the age when most people are in retirement, I took up a new career as a painter. Unable to do my farm chores at the age of 78 (1938), I began copying Currier and Ives prints and post cards. Once I mastered these, I began painting my own farm scenes and landscapes to preserve our rich, rural culture for future generations. I always worked from memory, sitting by the window of my upstairs bedroom. My use of color and composition began attracting attention in 1939, when some of my paintings were on display at the Museum of Modern Art (New York City). The following year, I had my own one-woman show with 35 of my paintings. Over the years, I painted 1,000 paintings. My most outstanding works include: "The Old Oaken Bucket, Sugaring Off" (1939), "Black Horses" (1941), "Catching the Thanksgiving Turkey" (1943), and "From My Window" (1946).

I was born on August 7, 1860, in Greenwich (Washington County), New York. When I was a child, my father would bring home blank sheets of newspaper for us to draw on. I liked to draw pictures and showed a great talent for it. My father encouraged my efforts, but my mother thought I was wasting my time when I could be doing something more useful. I left the farm in my early teens to become a hired girl at several farms. Then I married and we bought a farm in Eagle Bridge, New York. I worked the farm until my hands became crippled with arthritis. Looking for something to fill my time, I turned to oil painting. I died on December 13, 1961, in Hoosick Falls, New York.

WHO AM I?

1. I was born on August 7, 1860, in Greenwich, New York.
2. My use of color and composition began attracting attention while some of my works were on display at the Museum of Modern Art (1939).

3. In 1940, I had my own one-woman show with 35 of my paintings.
4. Over the years, I painted 1,000 paintings, including "The Oaken Bucket, Sugaring Off" (1939).
5. At the age when most people are in retirement (78), I took up a new career as a painter.

3 My first real success came in the early 1960s, when I emerged as a leader in the avant-garde pop art movement. This success was attributed to my silk-screen reproductions of Campbell soup cans, soft drink bottles, and soap-pad boxes. I also found success with portraits of public figures (e.g., Marilyn Monroe, Elizabeth Taylor, Elvis Presley, Jacqueline Kennedy, and Troy Donahue), pictures of the prison electric chair at Sing Sing, and various news events (e.g., race riots). In the 1960s, I also dabbled in film-making, with a series of experimental films such as *Kiss* (1963) and *Chelsea Girls* (1966, the most successful), and rock 'n' roll, recording one group, the Velvet Underground. I died on February 22, 1987, in New York City, New York.

I was born on August 6, 1927, in Philadelphia, Pennsylvania. As a child, my interest in pictures first showed itself in comic books, then in pictures of my own. Later, I studied art at the Carnegie Institute of Technology (Pittsburgh, Pennsylvania) and worked at the Joseph Horne store as a window decorator. Seeking a career in art, I moved to New York and found work as a successful illustrator for various advertisements in the early 1950s. In 1957, I received the Director's Club Medal for a shoe advertisement I had created. Four years later, I received recognition for a Lord & Taylor window display that featured Dick Tracy comic strip blow-ups. This led to other blow-ups (telephones and typewriters) and mass-produced silk-screens.

WHO AM I?

1. I was born on August 6, 1927, in Philadelphia, Pennsylvania.
2. I studied art at the Carnegie Institute of Technology.
3. In 1957, I won the Director's Club Medal for a shoe advertisement I had created.
4. I found success with portraits of public figures, including Marilyn Monroe, Elizabeth Taylor, and Elvis Presley.
5. My first real success came in the early 1960s, with my silk-screen reproductions of Campbell soup cans, soft drink bottles, and soap-pad boxes.

As an abstract painter, my paintings focused on natural objects (e.g., bones, flowers, rocks, and clouds), using close-ups or unusual vantage points to reduce them to their simplest form. To emphasize the abstractness of the paintings, I used thin paints (obliques) and clear colors to achieve a simple, abstract, Oriental style. My two most successful paintings of this period include: "Black Iris" (1926) and "Black Flower and Blue Larkspur" (1929). This same period produced several paintings of New York City and the East River. Afer spending the summer of 1929 in New Mexico, I began to focus my attention on the black landscapes, flowers, broad skies, horizon lines, cow skulls, and bare bones of the desert. Then in 1959, after taking an airplane trip around the world, my focus changed to the clouds I saw out my window. I used this new motif in 1966, for my largest work of all, a 24-foot mural of clouds.

I was born on November 15, 1887, in Sun Prairie, Wisconsin. At the age of 17, I went to study art at the Art Institute of Chicago (made drawings for advertisements) and later at the Art Student's League (won a prize for my class still life) in New York (1904–1908). The summer of 1912, I studied under Arthur Dow, who introduced me to Oriental art. That same year, I moved to Texas, where I taught school (art) for six years (1912–1918). While in Texas (1916) I sent some of my drawings to a New York friend, who showed them to Alfred Stieglitz (whom I later married), a photographer and owner of the 291 Gallery. He put the pictures on display in his gallery. In 1918, I moved back to New York where Stieglitz introduced me to his inner circle of painters. On January 29, 1923, I gained my first big success with an exhibition (called "One Hundred Pictures") at the Anderson Galleries.

WHO AM I?

1. I was born on November 15, 1887, in Sun Prairie, Wisconsin.
2. At the age of 17, I went to study art at the Art Institute of Chicago.
3. On January 29, 1923, I gained my first big success with an exhibition (called "One Hundred Pictures") at the Anderson Galleries.
4. My two most successful paintings are: "Black Iris" (1926) and "Black Flower and Blue Larkspur" (1929).
5. My abstract paintings focused on natural objects (e.g., bones, flowers, rocks, and clouds), using close-ups or unusual vantage points to reduce them to their simplest form.

5

I am considered one of the best-known American painters of the 20th century. My paintings reflect the rural areas around my winter home in Pennsylvania and the seashore around my summer home in Maine. My simple, familiar landscapes of russet, tan, green, brown, red, and light blue, along with the themes of forests, sea, sky, the hunter, life, and death, continually appeal to the public's senses. Some of my best-known paintings include: "Early Morning" (1943), "Blackberry Picker" (1943, best painting of the 1943 show at the Macbeth Galleries), "The Skaters" (1945, won the American Watercolor Society's Obrig Award), "Winter 1946" (1946), "Christina's World" (1948, best-known), and "Spool Bed" (1948). Earlier in 1947, I won a Merit Medal from the American Academy of Arts and Letters.

I was born on July 12, 1917, in Chadds Ford, Pennsylvania. When I was still young, my father (a well-known artist and illustrator in his own right) gave me art instruction after being impressed by a toy theater that I had designed. Because of poor health as a child, I was confined at home and educated by my parents and tutors, which also allowed me plenty of time to draw. At the age of 12, my father used some of my pen-and-ink drawings for a book he had illustrated. One of my father's students (Peter Hurd) was instrumental in teaching me the tempera technique. By the age of 20, I had my own one-man show at the Macbeth Gallery (New York), which featured only my watercolors. To my surprise, every painting sold.

WHO AM I?

1. I was born on July 12, 1917, in Chadds Ford, Pennsylvania.
2. When I was only 12, my father used some of my pen-and-ink drawings for a book that he had illustrated.
3. My paintings reflect the rural areas around my winter home (Pennsylvania) and the seashore by my summer home (Maine).
4. I used simple, familiar landscapes of russet, tan, green, and brown, with themes of forests, sea, sky, and life.
5. My best-known paintings include: "Early Morning" (1943), "Blackberry Picker" (1943), and "Christina's World" (1948).

6 By 1766, I had become a popular portrait painter at home and abroad. In 1765, I was admitted as a member of the Incorporated Society of Artists (later called the Royal Academy of Arts). Three years later, the king of England made me a charter member of the Society. The king gave me my first royal commission in 1769 ("The Departure of Regulars from Rome"), and in 1772 he made me his historical painter. My most successful works include: "Christ Healing the Sick" (1801),

"Christ Rejected" (1815), and "Death on the Pale Horse" (1817). My other works include: "Angelica and Medoro" (1764) and "The Return of the Prodigal Son" (1765–1767). I died on March 11, 1820, in London, England.

I was born on October 10, 1738, near Springfield, Pennsylvania. At an early age, I showed a talent for art and was encouraged by the elders of the Quaker church. When I was just six years old, I drew a sketch of my little niece. Two years later, a Philadelphia gentleman recognized my talent and bought me my first art supplies. When I was only 15, I was commissioned to do a portrait of Mrs. Ross of Lancaster, Pennsylvania. While living in Strawberry Alley, I painted portraits and signs for inns. Then I moved to Italy to study art (first American artist to do so) and later lived in England.

WHO AM I?

1. I was born on October 10, 1738, in Springfield, Pennsylvania.
2. At an early age, I showed a talent for art and was encouraged by the elders of the Quaker church.
3. The king of England gave me my first royal commission in 1769 ("The Departure of Regulars from Rome").
4. Some of my other works include: "Angelica and Medoro" (1764), "The Return of the Prodigal Son" (1765–1767), and "Death of Wolfe" (1771).
5. My most successful works include: "Christ Healing the Sick" (1801), "Christ Rejected" (1815), and "Death on the Pale Horse" (1817).

My first success came in 1782, with the painting "Portrait of a Gentleman Skating," which now enjoys international fame. After sending nine portraits to the Incorporated Society of Artists (Royal Academy) exhibit in 1783, they made me a member. Over the next five years, I painted many portraits with what I called transparent color, which gave them their life-like qualities. My most famous portraits include: "Benjamin West" (1781), "George Washington" (1794), "Thomas Jefferson" (1803), "Mrs. John Adams" (1815), and "James Monroe" (1817). Of the 1,000 portraits I painted, 124 were of George Washington. I died on July 9, 1828, in Boston, Massachusetts.

I was born on December 3, 1755, in North Kingstown Township (Kings County), in the Colony of Rhode Island and Providence Plantations. When I was 13, I began copying pictures and began drawing portraits in black lead. To perfect my talent, I went to study art with Cosmo Alexander in Edinburgh, Scotland. After his death, I was forced to work on a ship (1773–1774) headed for Novia Scotia. Finding no market for my paintings in the United States, I moved to London in 1775. In two years, I began contributing portraits (ten by 1782) to the Royal Academy exhibits. My popularity rose to the point that I was one of the most requested portrait painters in Europe.

WHO AM I?

1. I was born on December 3, 1755, in North Kingstown Township, in the Colony of Rhode Island.
2. When I was 13, I began copying pictures and began drawing portraits in black lead.
3. I painted many of my portraits with what I called transparent color, which gave them their life-like qualities.
4. My first success came in 1782, with the painting "Portrait of a Gentleman Skating."
5. My most famous portraits include: "Benjamin West" (1781), "George Washington" (1794; 124 portraits of him in all), "Thomas Jefferson" (1803), "Mrs. John Adams" (1815), and "James Monroe" (1817).

8   I am best remembered for my painting "American Gothic" (1930), a portrait of my sister and the local druggist standing in front of a white-gabled farmhouse. It won the Chicago Art Institute's Harris Award and remains the most copied painting today. My best-known works include: "Birthplace of Herbert Hoover" (1931), "Dinner for Threshers" (1934), "Death on Ridge Road" (1934), and "Parson Weems Fable" (1939). Other works include: pen-and-ink drawings for Sinclair Lewis' book "Main Street" (1920), "Woman with Plants" (1929), "John B. Turner – Pioneer" (1929), "Washington Crossing the Delaware" (1932), a Washington, DC post office mural (1934), and the landscapes "Young Corn" (1931) and "Arbor Day" (1932). I died of cancer on February 12, 1942, in Iowa City, Iowa.

My life began on February 13, 1892, on our farm near Anamosa, Iowa. After my father's death we moved to Cedar Rapids, where I worked odd jobs to support my family. While attending Washington High, I took a correspondence course in design and became involved with my school's and the Cedar Rapids Art Association's art projects. Then I spent two summers studying design and metalwork at the Minneapolis School of Design and Handicraft. The work came easily, and in 1917, I went into interior design. In 1923, I went to Paris to study art at the Académie Julian. Here I developed as an Impressionist painter.

WHO AM I?

1. My life began on February 13, 1892, in Anamosa, Iowa.
2. I spent two summers studying design and metalwork at the Minneapolis School of Design and Handicraft.
3. In 1923, I went to Paris to study art at the Académie Julian, where I developed as an Impressionist painter.
4. My best-known works include: "Birthplace of Herbert Hoover" (1931), "Midnight Ride of Paul Revere" (1931), "Death on Ridge Road" (1934), and "Parson Weems Fable" (1939).
5. I am best remembered for my painting "American Gothic" (1930), a portrait of my sister and a local druggist standing in front of a white-gabled farmhouse.

9

My lithographs were so popular that they continued to be printed for almost 70 years after they were first issued. The prints (over 7,000 different lithographs) depicted American life of the period (e.g., disasters, the California gold rush, politics, sports, and portraits of prominent Americans). The first print to gain local attention was the "Ruins of the Merchant's Exchange" (1835). My other prints include: "The Road—Winter" (1853), "Preparing for Market" (1856), "Life in the Country: The Morning Ride" (1859), "Central Park, Winter" (1859), and "Winter in the Country: Getting Ice" (1864). Earlier in the 1850s, I had gone into partnership with my bookkeeper, James Merritt Ives. I died of heart disease on November 20, 1888, in New York.

I was born on March 27, 1813, in Roxbury, Massachusetts. When I was 15, I apprenticed under William and John Pendleton in their Boston lithograph shop. Here I learned the business from the ground up. When John Pendleton left the business in 1829 to form a new lithograph house in Philadelphia, I followed him and remained there until 1833. The following year, I established my own lithograph business in New York. My company's first lithograph was "Ruins of the Planter's Hotel, New Orleans, Which Fell at Two O'clock on the Morning of the 15th of May 1835."

WHO AM I?

1. I was born on March 27, 1813, in Roxbury, Massachusetts.
2. When I was 15, I apprenticed under William and John Pendleton in their Boston lithograph shop.
3. My company's first lithograph was "Ruins of the Planter's Hotel, New Orleans, Which Fell at Two O'clock on the Morning of the 15th of May 1835."
4. Other prints include: "Ruins of the Merchant's Exchange" (1835), "Preparing for Market" (1856), and "Life in the Country: The Morning Ride" (1859).
5. I went into partnership with my bookkeeper, James Merritt Ives.

10   I am best-known as an Impressionist painter who depicted the theme of motherhood (e.g., "In the Omnibus," 1891 and "The Bath," 1891–1892) in almost every painting and print I did. The simple, quiet scenes of mothers and their babies in intimate, summer garden surroundings, captured the world's heart and the admiration of many. My works also include many portraits (e.g., "The Daughter of Alexander Cassatt," 1879), pastels and etchings. The latter brought raves from critics, who ranked me second behind Whistler as one of the best all-time etchers. My best-known paintings include: "The Blue Room" (1878), "A Woman in Black at the Opera" (1880), "Morning Toilette" (1886), and "The Boating Party" (1893). Later in life, I was forced to give up painting, because I was an invalid, almost blind. I died on June 14, 1926, in Paris, France. As a memorial tribute, the Pennsylvania Museum (Philadelphia) held an exhibition of my work (over 100 prints, 40 oils and pastels, and 15 watercolors and drawings) in April 1927.

My life began on May 22, 1845, in Allegheny City, Pennsylvania. After a trip to Paris with my mother in 1868, I decided to devote my life to art. Then I went on to study art in Parma, Italy, for eight months, and later in Spain. But my love of Paris drew me back (1874), and here I stayed for the rest of my life. Here I also set up a studio in the Rue de Marignan. After the painter Edgar Degas saw my work, he suggested that I exhibit my work at the Impressionist School, which I did for seven years (1879–1886). In 1893, my popularity grew with my first one-woman show at the Durard-Ruel (Paris). This show led to my selection (out of numerous American woman artists) to decorate the Women's Building in the Chicago Exhibit, and my selection as honorary president of "Hostel" for Girl Students in Paris. I won many medals and honors during my lifetime, which did not mean as much to me as my paintings did.

WHO AM I?

1. My life began on May 22, 1845, in Allegheny City, Pennsylvania.
2. After a trip to Paris with my mother in 1868, I decided to devote my life to art.
3. The critics ranked me second behind Whistler as one of the best all-time American etchers.
4. My best-known paintings include: "The Blue Room" (1878), "Morning Toilette" (1886), and "The Boating Party" (1893).
5. I am best-known as an Impressionist painter who depicted the theme of motherhood in almost every painting and print I did.

My paintings and sculptures of Westerns and Western scenery made me a popular artist of cowboy and Indian life. Two of my works in this vein are "In Without Knocking" (1908) and "Running Buffalo" (1918). In those earlier years, merchants and saloon-keepers displayed my work in their establishments, where my paintings sold well. This success led to my pictures being published in noteworthy Eastern magazines, then exhibited at the 1904 World's Fair in St. Louis, later in New York City, and also on calendars. Branching out into sculpture, I began casting small Western figures in wax. By 1904, I had cast them in bronze (100 figures in all), and Tiffany & Co. of New York sold them to the public.

I was born on March 19, 1864, in St. Louis, Missouri. My love of the Western outdoors began at an early age when I left home at 16 to become a cowboy in Montana. Here I photographed Indians, cowboys on cattle drives, and frontier life on the range. With the encouragement of my wife, Nancy Cooper (we were married in 1896), I forged a career as an artist. Later, we moved to Great Falls, Montana, where I set up an art studio. By the 1920s, my paintings were fetching $10,000 a piece. I died on October 24, 1926, in Great Falls, Montana.

WHO AM I?

1. I was born on March 19, 1864, in St. Louis, Missouri.
2. I left home at the age of 16 to become a cowboy.

3. In those early years, merchants and saloonkeepers displayed my work in their establishments.
4. Branching out into sculpture, I began casting small Western figures in wax. By 1904, I had cast them in bronze.
5. My paintings and sculptures of Western scenery made me a popular artist of cowboy and Indian life.

| 12 | My watercolors and paintings made me one of the most popular and famous painters of my day. The central theme of my watercolors was the sea: "The Fog Warning" (1885), "The Herring Net" (1885), |

"Eight Bells" (1886), "Early Morning After Storm at Sea" (1902, marked a turning point in my career), and "A Voice from the Cliffs" (1908). Another theme of my paintings was the battle of Yorktown: "Sharpshooter on Picket Duty" (1862), "The Last Goose at Yorktown" (1863), "Home, Sweet Home" (1863), and "Prisoners from the Front" (1866, the best of the bunch). My other works include: "The Morning Bell" (1866), "Croquet Scene" (1866), "The Two Guides" (1876), "Breezing Up" (1876), "Hark! the Lark" (1887), "Girl by the Seacoast" (1888), and "Fox Hunt" (1893). I died on September 29, 1910, at the height of my popularity.

I was born on February 24, 1836, in Boston, Massachusetts. At the age of 11, I enjoyed drawing sketches at the Washington Grammar School. By the time I was 19, my father had gotten me an apprenticeship with a lithographer in Boston. I apprenticed there for two years. With the help of my older brother, who supported me in my early years and had made a fortune as a chemist, I opened a studio on Winter Street. Here I secured my first work for *Ballou's Pictorial* and sold drawings in *Harper's Weekly* beginning in 1858. The following year, I moved to New York, where I set up a studio and studied art at the National Academy of Design. My first big break came in 1861, when Harper & Brothers hired me to make drawings of Abraham Lincoln's inauguration in Washington, DC.

WHO AM I?

1. I was born on February 24, 1836, in Boston, Massachusetts.

2. By the time I was 19, my father had gotten me an apprenticeship with a lithographer in Boston.
3. I secured my first work for *Ballou's Pictorial* and sold drawings in *Harper's Weekly* beginning in 1858.
4. Some of my works include: "Croquet Scene" (1866), "The Morning Bell" (1866), "Breezing Up" (1876), "Girl by the Seacoast" (1888), and "Fox Hunt" (1893).
5. The central theme of my watercolors was the sea: "The Fog Warning" (1885), "The Herring Net" (1885), "Eight Bells" (1886), and "A Voice from the Cliffs" (1908).

Chapter Twelve
Heroes of the Olympic Games

1

In the 1960 Olympic Games in Rome, Italy, I became the first American woman to win three gold medals in the running events. I won my first gold medal in the women's 100-meter dash, in which I tied the world record of 11.3 seconds in an earlier heat. My second gold medal came in the women's 200-meter dash, with a new Olympic record of 23.2 seconds. The third gold medal came as a member of the women's 400-meter relay team, in which I anchored the team to a world record time of 44.4 seconds. For my efforts, I was named America's Female Athlete of the Year (1960, voted by the Associated Press) and was voted the runner-up to Rafer Johnson (1960 Olympic decathlon champion) for the Amateur Athletic Union's 1960 Sullivan Award for Outstanding Amateur Athlete of the Year.

I was born (weighing only 4½ pounds) on June 23, 1940, in St. Bethlehem, Tennessee. My childhood was filled with illnesses and trials; at the age of four, double pneumonia and scarlet fever left my left leg useless, and at the age of eight, after years of physical therapy and massages, I was able to walk with special walking shoes. Through the dedication of my mother, I was able to walk on my own (without special shoes) at the age of 11. Later (14 years old), at Burt High School (an all-black school), I excelled in basketball and track. As a sophomore, I scored 803 points in 25 basketball games for a new state record. For three straight years in the outdoor track season, I won every race I entered. After graduation in June 1957, I went on to Tennessee State University.

WHO AM I?

1. I was born on June 23, 1940, in St. Bethlehem, Tennessee.

2. At the age of eight, after years of physical therapy and massages, I was able to walk with special walking shoes.
3. As a sophomore in high school, I scored 803 points in 25 basketball games for a new state record.
4. I was voted the runner-up to Rafer Johnson for the Amateur Athletic Union's 1960 Sullivan Award.
5. In the 1960 Olympic Games, I became the first American woman to win three gold medals in the running events.

2   At the 1968 Olympic Games in Mexico City, I defeated Ionas Cepulis of the Soviet Union to win the heavyweight gold medal. The following year, I turned professional and made my professional debut on June 23, 1969, at Madison Square Garden in New York, against Donald Waldheim (knockout in the 2nd round). I went on to defeat 32 opponents over the next two and a half years. On January 22, 1973, in Jamaica, I defeated Joe Frazier (knocked him down six times before the referee ended the fight) for the world heavyweight championship title. I successfully defended the title twice; first against Joe Roman (September 1, 1973, in Tokyo, Japan) and then against Ken Norton (March 26, 1974, in Caracus, Venezuela). Before the Norton fight transpired, I had an impressive undefeated professional record of 39 victories (36 by knockouts).

I was born (nicknamed "Monkey" as a baby) on January 10, 1949, in Marshall, Texas. We moved to Houston, where I spent my childhood wandering the streets looking for my next fight. After trying my hand at football (tackle, E.O. Smith Junior High School) and basketball (Hestor House), I switched to boxing while working for the Job Corps at Camp Parks. Here I took boxing instruction from Nick (Doc) Broadus who not only taught me the fundamentals, but involved me in a regular training routine. On January 26, 1967, at the San Francisco Golden Gloves Championship, I recorded a first-round knockout in my first official amateur fight. The following year, I won the National Amateur Athletic Union's boxing championship.

WHO AM I?

1. I was born on January 10, 1949, in Marshall, Texas.

2. On January 26, 1967 (San Francisco Golden Gloves Championship), I recorded a first-round knockout for my first win.
3. The following year, I won the National Amateur Athletic Union's boxing championship to qualify for the 1968 Olympics.
4. At the 1968 Olympic Games in Mexico City, I defeated Ionas Cepulis (Soviet Union) to win the heavyweight gold medal.
5. On January 22, 1973, I defeated Joe Frazier for the world heavyweight championship title.

3

My gold medal in women's figure skating at the 1968 Winter Olympics in Grenoble, France, was the only gold medal the United States received in February 1968. I defeated Gabriele Seyfert by 88.2 points, with a total score of 1,970.5 points. Three weeks later at the World Championship in Geneva, I retained my world title (for the third consecutive time) by scoring 2,179.8 points. Shortly before the Olympics, I had won my fifth consecutive United States National Championship. At just 19 years old, I announced my retirement from amateur skating competition on March 2, 1968. That same year, I signed a contract to appear on several television specials and went on to appear with the Ice Capades. Today, I do television commentary for various skating events, with my former guidance coach Dick Button.

I was born on July 27, 1948, in San Jose, California. At the age of nine, I laced on a pair of skates and began skating naturally. My father encouraged my talent and worked overtime to pay for my lessons so I could become a world champion, while my mother made all my skating costumes. By the time I was 11, I had started skating in competitions in Pasadena, California. The following year, in 1960 (12 years old), I won my first title at the Pacific Coast Juvenile Figure Skating Championship. The Pacific Coast Novice Ladies Championship followed in 1961. In 1963, I moved up to the senior ladies division of the Pacific Coast Championship and won the title. On January 11, 1964 (15 years old), I won my first women's national senior title, which qualified me for a spot on the 1964 United States Olympic skating team (finished 6th in the Olympics that year).

WHO AM I?

1. I was born on July 27, 1948, in San Jose, California.

2. At the age of 12, I won my first title at the Pacific Coast Juvenile Figure Skating Championship.
3. In 1971 at the World Championship in Geneva, I retained my world title (for the third time) by scoring 2,179.8.
4. My gold medal in women's figure skating at the 1968 Winter Olympics was the only gold medal the United States received that February.
5. I went on to appear with the Ice Capades. Today, I do television commentary on skating events with Dick Button.

4

In my day, I excelled in track, football, and baseball, and was considered one of the best all-time athletes. At the 1912 Olympic Games in Stockholm, Sweden, I won a gold medal in both the decathlon (10-events) and pentathlon (5-events); the feat has never been equaled.

I won the decathlon by scoring 8,412 points out of a possible 10,000 points, for a new world record. In the pentathlon, I placed first in four of the five events. Later, the International Olympic Committee forced me to return my gold medals when they found out that I had played professional baseball (for $15 a week for the semi-pro teams of Fayetteville and Rocky Mount).

For my efforts, I was inducted into both the college and professional Football Halls of Fame. I died on March 28, 1953, in Lomita, California. In 1983, the International Olympic Committee restored my medals and records.

I was born (tribal name "Bright Path") on May 28, 1888, in Shawnee, Oklahoma. At the Carlisle Indian School (five years) in Pennsylvania, I excelled in football as both a runner and kicker. In one game against Harvard, I kicked four field goals (23, 45, 37, and 48 yards) and scored a touchdown to single-handedly defeat them 18 to 15. The following year (1912), I scored 25 touchdowns and 198 points. From 1913 to 1919, I played professional baseball as an outfielder for the New York Giants, Cincinnati Reds, and Boston Braves, and had a .252 batting average in 289 games.

I also played professional football for seven different teams, including the New York Giants. Then in 1920, I became the first president of the American Professional Football Association. I spent my later years playing small parts in Westerns.

WHO AM I?

1. I was born on May 28, 1888, in Shawnee, Oklahoma.
2. At the Carlisle Indian School in Pennsylvania, I excelled in football as both a runner and kicker.
3. I played professional baseball (New York Giants, Cincinnati Reds, and Boston Braves) and football (7 different teams).
4. In the 1912 Olympic Games, I won a gold medal in both the decathlon and the pentathlon; the feat has never been equaled.
5. The International Olympic Committee forced me to return my gold medals when they had found out that I had played professional baseball (medals were restored in 1983).

5   At the 1936 Olympic Games in Berlin, Germany, I won four gold medals: the 100-meter dash (10.3 seconds, new Olympic record), 200-meter dash (20.7 seconds, new Olympic record), long jump (26 feet, 5½ inches, new Olympic record), and as a member of the 400-meter relay team (39.8 seconds, new world record). Earlier in 1935, as a member of the Ohio State University track team, I established three new world records in the 220-yard dash (20.3 seconds), 220-yard low hurdles (22.6 seconds), and the long jump (26 feet, 9 inches, becoming the first American to jump over 26 feet). In 1976, President Gerald R. Ford honored me with the Presidential Medal of Freedom, and in 1979 President Jimmy Carter honored me with a Living Legends Award. I died on March 31, 1980, in Tucson, Arizona.

I was born James Cleveland on September 12, 1913, in Danville, Alabama. As a child, I worked in the cotton fields, which built up my stamina for things to come. At Fairview Junior High (Cleveland), I established a new junior high school record by running the 100-yard dash in 10 seconds. Then at East Technical High School, I became a nationally recognized sprinter. I went on to star at Ohio State University, and at the 1933 National Interscholastic Championship I won the 100-yard dash (9.4 seconds), 200-yard dash (20.7 seconds), and the broad jump (24 feet, 9 5/8 inches). Here I was given the nicknames of "Brown Bombshell" and the "Buckeye Bullet." After the 1936 Olympics I was forced to work as a playground janitor and race against horses and dogs in degrading exhibition races.

WHO AM I?

1. I was born on September 12, 1913, in Danville, Alabama.
2. At Fairview Junior High School, I established a new junior high school record in the 100-yard dash (10 seconds).
3. In 1976, President Gerald R. Ford honored me with the Presidential Medal of Freedom.
4. At Ohio State University, as a member of the track team, I was given the nicknames "Brown Bombshell" and "Buckeye Bullet."
5. I won four gold medals (100-meter dash, 200-meter dash, long jump, and 400-meter relay) at the 1936 Olympic Games in Berlin, Germany.

6 At the 1984 Summer Olympic Games in Los Angeles (August 2nd), I won one gold (all-around), two silver (vault and team competition), and two bronze (floor exercise and uneven bars) medals, with an assortment of perfect 10s. In the all-around competition, I narrowly defeated Ecaterina Szabo, 79.175 to 79.125 for the gold. And I was the only gymnast to make the finals in all four events. Earlier, I had won a spot on the eight-member team at the Olympic trails in Jacksonville, Florida, with a first place overall finish (9.85 for the vault and floor exercises, 9.75 for the uneven bars, and 9.60 for the beam). Earlier that same year (March 1984), I once again won the American Cup all-around crown (39.5 points out of 40.0). From January 2, 1983, with Bela Karolyi as my coach, I was virtually undefeated until my retirement in 1986.

I was born on January 24, 1968, in Fairmont, West Virginia. When I was four years old, my mother signed me and my older sister up for ballet, tap, and acrobatic classes at Monica's Dance Studio. I was a quick study and quickly mastered basic acrobatic skills. The following year, my sister and I were taking gymnastic classes at West Virginia University. My progression was rapid, and soon I was enrolled in a gymnastic school (Aerialport, 1975) with Gary Rafaloski as one of my coaches; he coached me for seven years. When I was only eight years old, I won the Class III (beginner's) title at a statewide meet. At St. Anthony's school, I was not only involved in gymnastics, but I was also a Pee Wee cheerleader and homecoming queen, Pop Warner majorette, and track-and-field competitor.

WHO AM I?

1. I was born on January 24, 1968, in Fairmont, West Virginia.
2. When I was four years old, my mother signed me up for ballet, tap, and acrobatic classes at Monica's Dance Studio.
3. When I was only eight years old, I won the Class III (beginner's title) at a statewide meet.
4. In March 1984, I once again won the American Cup all-around crown (39.5 points out of 40.0).
5. At the 1984 Olympic Games, I won one gold (all-around), two silver (vault and team competition), and two bronze (floor exercise and uneven bars) medals; perfect 10s abounded.

7

In the 1984 Summer Olympic Games in Los Angeles, California, I won gold medals in both the springboard and platform diving events (the first man in 56 years to accomplish this feat). I had won the springboard event with 754.41 points, an astounding point total. Then I won the platform over fellow American Bruce Kimball with an unprecedented 710.91 points (became the first platform diver to score over 700 points), 70 points more than Bruce. Later, at the 1988 Summer Olympic Games in Seoul, South Korea, I repeated the feat by winning the springboard with 730.80 points and the platform with 638.61 points. Earlier, at the 1976 Summer Olympic Games in Montreal, Canada, I won a silver medal (23.52 points behind first) in the platform (at the age of 16). I am also the only diver in history to score straight perfect 10s in international competition. In 1985, I received the Amateur Athletic Union's Sullivan Award for Outstanding Amateur Athlete of the Year. The following year, I set a record by winning 38 national diving titles.

I was born on January 29, 1960, in El Cajon, California. My adoptive parents (adopted at nine months old) encouraged me to take dancing lessons at the age of two with my adopted sister. When I was nine, I turned to diving and, under the advice of a doctor, I also took up gymnastics to cure my asthma. When my father saw me practicing my tumbling routines off the diving board of our backyard swimming pool, he signed me up for diving classes at the La Mesa Parks and Recreation Center. In 1971, I scored a perfect 10 at the AAU Junior Olympics in Colorado Springs. Four years later, my father asked Dr. Sammy Lee (1948 and 1952 Olympic gold medalist in the 10-meter platform diving event) to coach me for the upcoming 1976 Olympics, which he did for free. I followed up my success at the Olympics with my first world titles in highboard diving (1978 and 1979) at the Pan-American Games, where I won gold medals in both the springboard and platform diving events.

WHO AM I?

1. I was born on January 29, 1960, in El Cajon, California.
2. My adoptive parents encouraged me to take dancing lessons at the age of two with my adopted sister.
3. When I was nine, I turned to diving, and under the advice of a doctor, I also took up gymnastics to cure my asthma.
4. In 1985, I received the Amateur Athletic Union's Sullivan Award for Outstanding Athlete of the Year.
5. I won two gold medals at the 1984 Olympic Games (springboard and platform diving events), and repeated the feat at the 1988 Olympic Games. I also won a silver medal (platform) in 1976.

8 My four gold medals at the 1984 Summer Olympic Games in Los Angeles, California, equaled Jesse Owens' record four gold medals at the 1936 Summer Olympics. I earned my gold medals in the 100-meters (9.9 seconds), 200-meters (19.80 seconds, new Olympic record), long jump (28 feet, ¼ inches), and the 4 × 400-meters relays (37.83 seconds, new Olympic record). That same year, I was drafted in the 12th round of the National Football League draft by the Dallas Cowboys; the Chicago Bulls of the National Basketball Association held my rights. I turned both teams down. Earlier (August 1983) at the World Championships in Helsinki, Finland, I won three gold medals for the 100-meters (10.07 seconds), long jump (fraction over 28 feet), and 400-meters relay (37.86, new world record). In 1981, I was honored with the Amateur Athletic Union's Sullivan Award for Outstanding Athlete of the Year.

I was born Frederick Carlton on July 1, 1961, in Birmingham, Alabama. When I was just eight years old, I began running track for the Willingboro Track Club (a club my parents founded). Four years later (1973),

I participated in the Jesse Owens Youth Programs meet (Philadelphia, Pennsylvania) and took first place in the long jump with a leap of 17 feet, 6 inches. In 1978, I established new national high school records in the 100-yard dash (9.3 seconds) and long jump (25 feet, 9 inches). My final year in high school, I was named All-American in the 200-meters and long jump and was ranked the number one high school track athlete in the nation. After graduation, I attended the University of Houston on an athletic scholarship (majored in communications). By the end of 1986, I had won 48 consecutive long jump competitions.

WHO AM I?

1. I was born on July 1, 1961, in Birmingham, Alabama.
2. When I was just eight years old, I began running track for the Willingboro Track Club (a club my parents founded).
3. In 1978, I established new national high school records in the 100-yard dash (9.3 seconds) and long jump (25 feet, 9 inches); I was named All-American in the 200-meters and long jump.
4. At the World Championships in Helsinki, I won three gold medals for the 100-meters, long jump, and 400-meters relay.
5. My four gold medals at the 1984 Olympic Games equaled Jesse Owens' record four gold medals at the 1936 Olympics.

9 I made history at the 1972 Olympic Games in Munich, West Germany, by winning a record seven gold medals. My first gold came in the 200-meter butterfly (2 minutes, ⁷⁄₁₀ of a second, new world record). The next six gold medals came in the 400-meter freestyle relay (3 minutes, 26.42 seconds, new world record), 200-meter freestyle (1 minute, 52.78 seconds), 100-meter butterfly (54.27 seconds, new world record), anchored the 800-meter freestyle relay (7 minutes, 35.78 seconds, new world record), 100-meter freestyle (51.22 seconds), and 400-meter medley relay (3 minutes, 48.16 seconds, new world record). Earlier, at the 1968 Olympic Games in Mexico City, I won two golds as a member of two relay teams and individual silver and bronze medals. For my efforts, I won the Amateur Athletic Union's Sullivan Award for Outstanding Athlete of the Year (1971) and the World Swimmer of the Year (1967 and 1971).

My life began on February 10, 1950, in Modesto, California. When I was just barely able to walk, my parents had me swimming in the pool. By the time I was eight, they had enrolled me in a swimming class at the YMCA in Sacramento, California. The following year, my father arranged for me to swim under the guidance of Sherman Chavoor. Under his instruction (at the age of ten), I held 17 national records for my age group. Four years later (at the age of 14), I qualified for the National AAU Championships. In 1967, I won five gold medals (set five world records in the process for freestyle and butterfly) in the Pan-American Games. After graduating from Santa Clara High School in 1968, I went on to the University of Indiana (1969–1972), where I was a member of four national championship teams. During my swimming career I set a total of 35 world records.

WHO AM I?

1. My life began on February 10, 1950, in Modesto, California.
2. When I was just barely able to walk, my parents had me swimming in the pool.
3. In 1967, I won five gold medals (set five world records in freestyle and butterfly) in the Pan-American games.
4. I won two golds as a member of two relay teams and individual silver and bronze medals at the 1968 Olympic Games.
5. At the 1972 Olympic Games, I made history by winning a record seven gold medals.

10

At the 1968 Summer Olympic Games in Mexico City, I set a world record in the long jump with a leap of 29 feet, 2½ inches to capture the gold medal. Earlier that year, I set an indoor world long jump record of 27 feet, 1 inch, and won the United States indoor title with a leap of 27 feet, 4 inches. At the United States Olympic trials, I jumped 27 feet, 6½ inches, but was disqualified because wind conditions figured prominently in the jump. I eventually qualified for the Olympics with a leap of 26 feet, 10½ inches. My prowess as a sprinter (9.5 seconds for 100 meters) and high jumper (6 feet, 5 inches) contributed to my success as a long jumper. Going into the Olympic trials, I had a string of 22 victories (indoor and outdoor). For my efforts, I was named Outstanding Athlete of 1968 by *Track and Field News*.

I was born on August 29, 1946, in Jamaica, New York. While attending Jamaica High School (Long Island, New York), I played basketball and, as a senior, averaged 20 points per game. After graduation I briefly attended North Carolina Agricultural and Technical College (Greensboro), then went on to the University of Texas at El Paso, where I built up a string of victories in the long jump. After the Olympics I transferred to Adelphi University, where I played basketball and was a member of the track team. I also competed in the International Track Association (founded in 1973) to promote professional track-and-field events.

WHO AM I?

1. I was born on August 29, 1946, in Jamaica, New York.
2. While attending Jamaica High School, I played basketball and, as a senior, averaged 20 points per game.
3. My prowess as a sprinter (9.5 seconds for 100 meters) and high jumper (6 feet, 5 inches) contributed to my success as a long jumper.
4. In 1968, I set an indoor world long jump record of 27 feet, 1 inch, and won the United States indoor title.
5. At the 1968 Olympics, I set a world record in the long jump with a leap of 29 feet, 2½ inches to capture the gold.

11

At the 1960 Summer Olympic Games in Rome, Italy, I won the gold medal in the decathlon by narrowly defeating C.K. Yang. I also carried the American flag in the opening ceremonies. Before the 1960 Olympics, I had badly injured my back in an automobile accident that made it impossible for me to train for a year and a half; winning the gold was extra special for me that year. Earlier, at the 1956 Summer Olympic Games (Melbourne, Australia), I won a silver medal in the decathlon. The year before, I was the fastest low-hurdler in the country, winner of the decathlon at the Pan-American Games, and broke Bob Mathias' world record for the decathlon (by 98 points) at the National AAU meet in Kingsbury.

I was born on August 18, 1935, in Hillsboro, Texas. By the time I was 15, I could long jump more than 21 feet. After watching Bob Mathias compete in a Tulare, California, track meet I became interested in the decathlon. While still in high school, I won two state decathlon events by high jumping 6 feet, 3 inches, running the hurdles in 14.3 seconds, throwing the shot put almost 52 feet, and long jumping 23 feet. As a high school senior, I finished third in the Amateur Athletic Union's (AAU) National Decathlon (Atlantic City, New Jersey). For my efforts, I won a track scholarship to UCLA in 1954. As a freshman, I tied the national hurdles record for freshmen with a time of 14 seconds.

WHO AM I?

1. I was born on August 18, 1935, in Hillsboro, Texas.
2. By the time I was 15, I could long jump more than 21 feet.
3. I won a track scholarship to UCLA in 1954, and tied the national hurdles record for freshman (14 seconds).
4. Later, at the 1956 Olympics, I won a silver in the decathlon.
5. Four years later at the 1960 Olympics, I won the gold medal in the decathlon by narrowly defeating C.K. Yang.

12

At the 1968 Olympic Games in Mexico City, I won three gold medals in women's swimming (despite a sprained ankle and the flu). The gold medals came in the 200-meter freestyle (2 minutes, 10.5 seconds, new Olympic record), 400-meter freestyle (4 minutes, 31.8 seconds, new Olympic record), and the 800-meter freestyle (9 minutes, 24.0 seconds, new Olympic record); that made me the first woman in Olympic history to win three gold medals in swimming. Earlier (July 1968), at the Los Angeles Invitational meet, I won the 1,500-meter freestyle (17 minutes, 31.2 seconds, new world record) and 800-meter freestyle (9 minutes, 19 seconds, new world record). For my efforts at the Olympic trials in August 1968, I won the Amateur Athletic Union's Sullivan Award for Outstanding Athlete of the Year.

My life began on August 14, 1952, in Annapolis, Maryland. With the encouragement of my parents, I began swimming seriously at the age of eight. Seeing my potential as a champion, my father obtained a transfer from his company to California, so I could train with the Olympic swimming coach, Sherman Chavoor. In July 1967 (15 years old), I set new world records in the women's 800- and 1,500-meter freestyle. That same month, I won the 400-meter freestyle (4 minutes, 32.6 seconds, new world record) and 800-meter freestyle (9 minutes, 22.9 seconds, new world record) at the Pan-American Games in Winnipeg, Canada. The next month at the National AAU Championship, I won the 400-meter freestyle (4 minutes, 29 seconds) and 1,500-meter freestyle (17 minutes, 50.2 seconds); both were new records breaking my previous records. For my efforts, I was named Sportswoman of 1967.

WHO AM I?

1. My life began on August 14, 1952, in Annapolis, Maryland.
2. With the encouragement of my parents, I began swimming seriously at the age of eight.
3. At the Pan-American Games in 1967, I won the 400-meter freestyle and the 800-meter freestyle, both in world record time.
4. In 1969, I won the Amateur Athletic Union's Sullivan Award for Outstanding Athlete of the Year.
5. At the 1968 Olympics, I won three gold medals in women's swimming. The gold medals came in the 200-meter freestyle, 400-meter freestyle, and the 800-meter freestyle; all of my times set new Olympic records.

Summary of Correct Answers, with Further Readings

Chapter One. Presidents

Answers: 1. Thomas Jefferson; 2. James Buchanan; 3. Franklin Delano Roosevelt; 4. John Fitzgerald Kennedy; 5. Ulysses S. Grant; 6. Woodrow Wilson; 7. James A. (Abram) Garfield; 8. Dwight D. (David) Eisenhower; 9. William Howard Taft; 10. Harry S Truman; 11. Abraham Lincoln; 12. William McKinley.

Brodie, Fawn M. *Thomas Jefferson, An Intimate History.* New York: W.W. Norton, 1974.

Cunningham, Noble E., Jr. *In Pursuit of Reason: The Life of Thomas Jefferson.* Baton Rouge: Louisiana State University Press, 1987.

Malone, Dumas. *Jefferson and His Times.* 6 vols. Boston: Little, Brown, 1981.

Klein, Philip Shriver. *President James Buchanan, A Biography.* University Park, Pennsylvania: Pennsylvania State University Press, 1962.

Smith, Elbert B. *The Presidency of James Buchanan.* Lawrence, Kansas: University Press of Kansas, 1975.

Targ-Brill, Marlene. *James Buchanan: Fifteenth President of the United States.* Chicago: Children's Press, 1988.

Alsop, Joseph. *FDR, 1882–1945: A Centenary Remembrance.* New York: Viking, 1982.

Davis, Kenneth S. *FDR: The Beckoning of Destiny, 1882–1928, A History.* New York: G.P. Putnam's Sons, 1972.

Miller, Nathan. *FDR, an Intimate History.* Garden City, New York: Doubleday, 1983.

Kennedy, John Fitzgerald. *Profiles in Courage.* New York: Franklin Watts, 1964.

Lichtenstein, Nelson, ed. *Political Profiles: The Kennedy Years.* New York: Facts on File, 1976.

Sorensen, Theodore C. *Kennedy.* New York: Harper & Row, 1965.

Catton, Bruce; ed. by Oscar Handlin. *U.S. Grant and the American Military Tradition*. Boston: Little, Brown and Company, 1954.

Korn, Jerry, and editors of Time-Life Books. *War on the Mississippi: Grant's Vicksburg Campaign*. Alexandria, Virginia: Time-Life Books, 1985.

Smith, Gene. *Lee and Grant, A Dual Biography*. New York: Promontory Press (distributed by Blue and Grey Press), 1984.

Farrell, Robert H. *Woodrow Wilson and World War I, 1917–1921*. New York: Harper & Row, 1985.

Shachtman, Tom. *Edith and Woodrow: A Presidential Romance*. Thorn, Maine: Thorndike, 1981.

Smith, Gene. *When the Cheering Stopped: The Last Years of Woodrow Wilson*. New York: Morrow, 1964.

Doenecke, Justus D. *The Presidencies of James A. Garfield and Chester A. Arthur*. Lawrence, Kansas: Regents Press of Kansas, 1981.

Lillegard, Dee. *James A. Garfield, Twentieth President of the United States*. Chicago: Children's Press, 1987.

Peskin, Allan. *Garfield: A Biography*. Kent, Ohio: Kent State University Press, 1978.

Eisenhower, David. *Eisenhower: At War 1943–45*. New York: Random House, 1986.

Eisenhower, Dwight D. *At Ease: Stories I Tell to Friends*. Garden City, New York: Doubleday, 1967.

Eisenhower, Dwight D. *Mandate for Change: The White House Years, A Personal Account*. Garden City, New York: Doubleday, 1963.

Black, Gilbert J.; ed. by Dobbs Ferry. *William Howard Taft, 1857–1930; Chronology, Documents, Bibliographical Aids*. New York: Oceana Publications, 1970.

Diller, Daniel C., and Stephen L. Robertson. *The Presidents, First Ladies, and Vice Presidents: White House Biographies 1789–1989*. Washington, DC: Congressional Quarterly, 1989, pp. 58–59.

Ross, Ishbel. *An American Family; The Tafts, 1678 to 1964*. Cleveland: World Publishing, 1964.

Miller, Merle. *Plain Speaking; An Oral Biography of Harry S Truman*. California: Berkley Publishing, 1974.

Steinberg, Alfred. *Harry S Truman*. New York: G.P. Putnam's Sons, 1963.

Truman, Margaret. *Harry S Truman*. New York: William Morrow & Company, 1973.

Angle, Paul M., ed. *The Lincoln Reader*. New Brunswick, New Jersey: Rutgers University Press, 1947.

Basler, Roy P., Marion Dolores Pratt, and Lloyd A. Dunlap, eds. *The Collected Works of Abraham Lincoln*. 8 vols. New Brunswick, New Jersey: Rutgers University Press, 1953.

Sandburg, Carl. *Abraham Lincoln: The Prairie Years*. 2 vols. *Abraham Lincoln: The War Years*. 4 vols. New York: Harcourt, Brace & World, 1926.

Gould, Lewis L. *The Presidency of William McKinley.* Lawrence, Kansas: Regents Press of Kansas, 1980.

Kent, Zachary. *William McKinley: Twenty-Fifth President of the United States.* Chicago: Children's Press, 1988.

Leech, Margaret. *In the Days of McKinley.* New York: Harper, 1959.

Chapter Two. Women

Answers: 1. Susan B. (Brownell) Anthony; 2. Amelia Earhart; 3. Clara (Clarissa Harlowe) Barton; 4. Betsy Ross; 5. Dorothea Lynde Dix; 6. Anna "Eleanor" Roosevelt; 7. Carrie (Amelia Moore Gloyd) Nation; 8. Molly (Mary Ludwig Hays McCauley) Pitcher; 9. Helen Keller; 10. Sally Kristen Ride; 11. Dorothy "Dolley" Payne Todd Madison; 12. Sandra Day O'Connor.

Barry, Kathleen. *Susan B. Anthony: A Biography of a Singular Feminist.* New York: New York University Press, 1988.

Cooper, Ilene. *Susan B. Anthony.* New York: F. Watts, 1984.

Weisberg, Barbara. *Susan B. Anthony.* New York: Chelsea House, 1988.

Goerner, Fred. *The Search for Amelia Earhart.* Garden City, New York: Doubleday, 1966.

Loomis, Vincent V., and Jeffrey L. Ethell. *Amelia Earhart: The Final Story.* New York: Random House, 1985.

Lovell, Mary S. *The Sound of Wings: The Life of Amelia Earhart.* New York: St. Martin's Press, 1989.

Hamilton, Leni. *Clara Barton.* New York: Chelsea House, 1988.

Klingel, Cindy. *Clara Barton, Red Cross Pioneer (1821–1912).* Mankato, Minnesota: Creative Education, 1987.

Pryor, Elizabeth Brown. *Clara Barton, Professional Angel.* Philadelphia: University of Pennsylvania Press, 1987.

Mayer, Jane Rothschild. *Betsy Ross and the Flag.* New York: Random House, 1952.

Parry, Edwin Satterthwaite. *Betsy Ross, Quaker Rebel: Being the True Story of the Romantic Life of the Maker of the First American Flag.* Chicago: The John Winston Company, 1930.

Weil, Ann. *Betsy Ross. Girl of Old Philadelphia.* Indianapolis: Bobbs-Merrill, 1954.

Marshall, Helen E. *Dorothea Dix: Forgotten Samaritan.* New York: Russell & Russell, 1967.

Melin, Grace Hathaway. *Dorothea Dix: Girl Reformer.* Indianapolis: Bobbs-Merrill, 1963.

Wilson, Dorothy Clarke. *Stranger and Traveler: The Story of Dorothea Dix, American Reformer.* Boston: Little, Brown, 1975.

Lash, Joseph P. *Eleanor Roosevelt, A Friend's Memoir.* New York: Doubleday, 1964.

Lash, Joseph P. *Love, Eleanor: Eleanor Roosevelt and Her Friends.* New York: Doubleday, 1982.

Roosevelt, Anna Eleanor. *The Autobiography of Eleanor Roosevelt.* New York: Harper & Brothers, 1961.

Asbury, Herbert. *Carry Nation.* New York: A.A. Knopf, 1929.

Beals, Carleton. *Cyclone Carry: The Story of Carry Nation.* Philadelphia: Chilton Company, 1962.

Taylor, Robert Lewis. *Vessel of Wrath: The Life and Times of Carry Nation.* New York: New American Library, 1966.

James, Edward T., ed. *Notable American Women: A Biographical Dictionary.* 11 vols. Cambridge, Massachusetts: The Belknap Press of Harvard University Press, 1975.

Stevenson, Augusta. *Molly Pitcher: Girl Patriot.* Indianapolis: Bobbs-Merrill, 1960.

The World Book Encyclopedia. vol. 15. Chicago: World Book, 1988, p. 505.

Gibson, William. *The Miracle Worker.* New York: Bantam Books, 1960.

Keller, Helen Adams. *Helen Keller: The Story of My Life.* Garden City, New York: Doubleday, 1954.

Lash, Joseph P. *Helen and Teacher: The Story of Helen Keller & Anne Sullivan Macy.* New York: Delacorte Press, 1980.

Blacknall, Carolyn. *Sally Ride, America's First Woman in Space.* Minneapolis, Minnesota: Dillion Press, 1984.

O'Connor, Karen. *Sally Ride and the New Astronauts: Scientists in Space.* New York: F. Watts, 1983.

Ride, Sally, and Susan Okie. *To Space and Back.* New York: Lothrop, Lee & Shepard, 1986.

Daugherty, Sonia Medviedeva. *Ten Brave Women.* New York: Lippincott, 1953.

Gerson, Noel Bertram. *The Velvet Glove.* Nashville: T. Nelson, 1975.

Mayer, Jane Rothschild. *Dolly Madison.* New York: Random House, 1954.

Fox, Mary Virginia. *Justice Sandra Day O'Connor.* Hillside, New Jersey: Enslow, 1983.

Huber, Peter W. *Sandra Day O'Connor.* New York: Chelsea House, 1990.

Woods, Harold, and Geraldine Woods. *Equal Justice: A Biography of Sandra Day O'Connor.* Minneapolis, Minnesota: Dillion Press, 1985.

Chapter Three. *African Americans*

Answers: 1. Frederick Douglass; 2. Harriet Tubman; 3. Martin Luther King, Jr; 4. Mary McLeod Bethune; 5. W.E.B. (William Edward Burghardt) DuBois; 6. Rosa Parks; 7. Booker T. (Taliaferro) Washington; 8. Thurgood Marshall; 9. Sojourner Truth; 10. George Washington Carver; 11. Ralph Abernathy; 12. Jesse Jackson.

Bontemps, Arna. *Free at Last: The Life of Frederick Douglass.* New York: Dodd, Mead, 1971.

Douglass, Frederick. *My Bondage and My Freedom*. Chicago: Johnson, 1970.

Douglass, Frederick; ed. by Philip S. Foner. *The Life and Writings of Frederick Douglass*. 5 vols. New York: International, 1950–1975.

Bradford, Sarah. *Harriet Tubman: The Moses of Her People*. Gloucester, Massachusetts: Peter Smith, 1981.

Conrad, Earl. *Harriet Tubman: Negro Soldier and Abolitionist*. Middlebury, Vermont: Eriksson, 1970.

Petry, Ann. *Harriet Tubman: Conductor on the Underground Railroad*. New York: Pocket Books, 1971.

Bishop, Jim. *The Days of Martin Luther King, Jr.* New York: G.P. Putnam's Sons, 1971.

King, Coretta Scott. *My Life with Martin Luther King, Jr.* New York: Holt, Rinehart & Winston, 1969.

King, Martin Luther, Jr. *Where Do We Go from Here: Chaos or Community?* New York: Harper & Row, 1967.

Anderson, LaVere. *Mary McLeod Bethune: Teacher with a Dream*. Champaign, Illinois: Garrard, 1976.

Halasa, Malu. *Mary McLeod Bethune*. New York: Chelsea House, 1989.

Hicks, Florence Johnson, ed. *Mary McLeod Bethune: Her Own Words of Inspiration*. Washington: Nuclassics & Science, 1975.

DuBois, W.E.B. *The Autobiography of W.E.B. DuBois: A Soliloquy on Viewing My Life from the Last Decade of Its First Century*. New York: International, 1968.

DuBois, W.E. Burghardt. *The Souls of Black Folk: Essays and Sketches*. New York: Dodd, Mead & Company, 1961.

Marble, Manning. *W.E.B. DuBois, Black Radical Democrat*. Boston: Twayne, 1986.

Greenfield, Eloise. *Rosa Parks*. New York: Crowell, 1973.

Meriwether, Louise. *Don't Ride the Bus on Monday: The Rosa Parks Story*. Englewood Cliffs, New Jersey: Prentice-Hall, 1973.

Stevenson, Janet. "Rosa Parks Wouldn't Budge." *American Heritage*, February 1972, pp. 56–64, 85.

Harlan, Louis R. *Booker T. Washington: The Making of a Black Leader*. New York: Oxford University Press, 1972.

Harlan, Louis R., ed. *The Booker T. Washington Papers*. Urbana, Illinois: University of Illinois Press, 1984.

Washington, Booker T. *Up from Slavery*. New York: Penguin Books, 1986.

Aldred, Lisa. *Thurgood Marshall*. New York: Chelsea House, 1990.

Bland, Randall Walton. *Private Pressure on Public Law: The Legal Career of Justice Thurgood Marshall*. Port Washington, New York: Kennikat Press, 1973.

Fenderson, Lewis H. *Thurgood Marshall: Fighter for Justice*. New York: McGraw-Hill, 1969.

Asher, Sandra Fenichel. *A Woman Called Truth*. Woodstock, Illinois: Dramatic, 1989.

Claflin, Edward Beecher. *Sojourner Truth and the Struggle for Freedom*. Chicago: Children's Press Choice, 1987.

Ferris, Jeri. *Walking the Road to Freedom: A Story About Sojourner Truth*. Minneapolis: Carolrhoda Books, 1988.

Adair, Gene. *George Washington Carver*. New York: Chelsea House, 1989.

McMurry, Linda O. *George Washington Carver: Scientist and Symbol*. New York: Oxford University Press, 1981.

Nabokov, Peter Towne. *George Washington Carver*. New York: Crowell, 1975.

Abernathy, Ralph David. *And the Walls Came Tumbling Down: An Autobiography*. New York: Harper & Row, 1989.

Abernathy, Ralph David. "Privacy for the Dead?" *National Review*, November 24, 1989, pp. 13–14.

"Abernathy, Ralph David." *Current Biography*, June 1990, p. 59.

Colton, Elizabeth O. *The Jackson Phenomenon: The Man. The Power. The Message*. New York: Doubleday, 1989.

McKissack, Patricia C. *Jesse Jackson: A Biography*. New York: Scholastic, 1989.

Otfinoski, Steven. *Jesse Jackson: A Voice for Change*. New York: Fawcett Columbine, 1990.

Chapter Four. Stars of the Silver Screen

Answers: 1. Mae West; 2. Bette Davis; 3. Lillian Gish; 4. Clark Gable; 5. Gloria Swanson; 6. Katharine Hepburn; 7. Marilyn Monroe; 8. Fred Astaire; 9. Judy Garland; 10. Grace Kelly; 11. Rita Hayworth; 12. Spencer Tracy.

Bergman, Carol. *Mae West*. New York: Chelsea House, 1987.

Musgrove, Eells, and Stanley Musgrove. *Mae West: A Biography*. New York: Morrow, 1982.

West, Mae. *Goodness Had Nothing to Do with It*. New York: Prentice-Hall, 1959.

Davis, Bette, with Michael Herskowitz. *This 'n That*. New York: Putnam's, 1987.

Moseley, Roy. *Bette Davis: An Intimate Memoir*. New York: D.I. Fine, 1990.

Stine, Whitney. *I'd Love to Kiss You . . . : Conversations with Bette Davis*. Thorndike, Maine: Thorndike Press, 1990.

Frasher, James E., ed. *Dorothy and Lillian Gish*. New York: Scribner, 1973.

Gish, Lillian, and Ann Pinchot. *Lillian Gish: The Movies, Mr. Griffith, and Me*. Englewood Cliffs, New Jersey: Prentice-Hall, 1969.

Gish, Lillian, and Selma G. Lanes. *An Actor's Life for Me*. New York: Viking Kestrel, 1987.

Jordan, Rene. *Clark Gable*. New York: Galahad Books, 1973.

Kobal, John, ed. *Clark Gable*. Boston: Little, Brown, 1986.

Scagnetti, Jack. *The Life and Loves of Gable*. New York: J. David, 1976.

Hudson, Richard M., and Raymond Lee. *Gloria Swanson*. South Brunswick: A.S. Barnes, 1970.

Quirk, Lawrence J. *The Films of Gloria Swanson*. Secaucus, New Jersey: Citadel Press, 1984.

Swanson, Gloria. *Swanson on Swanson: An Autobiography*. New York: Random House, 1980.

Andersen, Christopher. *Young Kate.* New York: Henry Holt, 1988.

Carey, Gary. *Katharine Hepburn: A Hollywood Yankee.* New York: St. Martin's, 1983.

Kanin, Garson. *Tracy and Hepburn: An Intimate Memoir.* New York: Viking Press, 1971.

Conway, Michael, and Mark Ricci. *The Films of Marilyn Monroe.* New York: Citadel, 1964.

Guiles, Fred Lawrence. *Norma Jean: The Life of Marilyn Monroe.* New York: McGraw, 1969.

Summers, Anthony. *Goddess: The Secret Lives of Marilyn Monroe.* New York: New American Library, 1986.

Adler, Bill. *Fred Astaire: A Wonderful Life.* New York: Carroll & Graf, 1987.

Giles, Sarah. *Fred Astaire: His Friends Talk.* New York: Doubleday, 1988.

Thomas, Bob, with comments by Fred Astaire. *Astaire. The Man, the Dancer: The Life of Fred Astaire.* New York: St. Martin's, 1984.

Edwards, Anne. *Judy Garland: A Biography.* New York: Simon and Schuster, 1975.

Frank, Gerold. *Judy.* New York: Harper & Row, 1975.

Watson, Thomas J., and Bill Chapman. *Judy, Portrait of an American Legend.* New York: McGraw-Hill, 1986.

Davis, Phyllida Hart. *Grace: The Story of a Princess.* New York: St. Martin's, 1982.

Englund, Steven. *Grace of Monaco.* Garden City, New York: Doubleday, 1984.

Spada, James. *Grace: The Secret Lives of a Princess.* Garden City, New York: Doubleday, 1987.

Hill, James. *Rita Hayworth. A Memoir.* New York: Simon and Schuster, 1983.

Leaming, Barbara. *If This Was Happiness: A Biography of Rita Hayworth.* New York: Viking Press, 1989.

Morella, Joe, and Edward Z. Epstein. *Rita. The Life of Rita Hayworth.* New York: Delacorte, 1983.

Davidson, Bill. *Spencer Tracy, Tragic Idol.* New York: Dutton, 1988.

Kanin, Garson. *Tracy and Hepburn: An Intimate Memoir.* New York: Viking Press, 1971.

Swindell, Larry. *Spencer Tracy: A Biography.* New York: World, 1969.

Chapter Five. Sports Figures

Answers: 1. Babe Ruth; 2. Althea Gibson; 3. Joe Louis; 4. Arnold Palmer; 5. Mildred "Babe" Didrikson Zaharias; 6. Muhammad Ali; 7. Joe DiMaggio; 8. Wilt Chamberlain; 9. Sugar Ray Robinson; 10. Billie Jean King; 11. Henry "Hank" Aaron; 12. Jim Brown.

Berke, Art. *Babe Ruth.* New York: F. Watts, 1988.

Creamer, Robert W. *Babe: The Legend Comes to Life.* New York: Simon and Schuster, 1974.

Smelser, Marshall. *The Life That Ruth Built: A Biography.* New York: Quadrangle, 1975.

Biracree, Tom. *Althea Gibson.* New York: Chelsea House, 1989.

Fitzgerald, Ed, ed. *I Always Wanted to Be Somebody.* New York: Harper, 1958.

Gibson, Althea, and Richard Curtis. *So Much to Live For.* New York: G.P. Putnam's Sons, 1968.

Barrow, Joe Louis, and Barbara Munder. *Joe Louis: 50 Years an American Hero.* New York: McGraw-Hill, 1988.

Jakoubek, Robert. *Joe Louis: Heavyweight Champion.* New York: Chelsea House, 1990.

Mead, Chris. *Champion, Joe Louis: Black Hero in White America.* New York: Scribner's Sons, 1985.

Bisher, Furman, and Murray Olderman, eds. *The Birth of a Legend: Arnold Palmer's Golden Year, 1960.* Englewood Cliffs, New Jersey: Prentice-Hall, 1972.

Palmer, Arnold. *Play Great Golf: Mastering the Fundamentals of Your Game.* Garden City, New York: Doubleday, 1987.

Palmer, Arnold, and William Barry. *Go for Broke: My Philosophy of Winning Golf.* New York: Simon and Schuster, 1973.

Lynn, Elizabeth A. *Babe Didrikson Zaharias.* New York: Chelsea House, 1989.

Schoor, Gene. *Babe Didrikson: The World's Great Woman Athlete.* Garden City, New York: Doubleday, 1978.

Zaharias, Babe Didrikson, and Harry Paxton. *This Life I've Led: My Autobiography.* New York: Barnes, 1955.

Ali, Muhammad, and Richard Durham. *The Greatest: My Own Story.* New York: Random House, 1975.

Hahn, James, and Lynn Hahn. *Ali!: The Sports Career of Muhammad Ali.* Mankato, Minnesota: Crestwood House, 1981.

Rummel, Jack. *Muhammad Ali.* New York: Chelsea House, 1988.

Berke, Art, and William Redding, eds. *The Lincoln Library of Sports Champions.* 14 vols. Columbus, Ohio: Sports Resources Company, 1974, pp. 46–53.

Halberstam, David. "The Great Joe D: An Excerpt from the New Book *Summer of '49.*" New York, May 8, 1989, pp. 42–52.

Seidel, Michael. *Streak: Joe DiMaggio and the Summer of '41.* New York: McGraw-Hill, 1988.

Chamberlain, Wilt, and David Shaw. *Wilt, Just Like Any Other 7-Foot Black Millionaire Who Lives Next Door.* New York: Macmillan, 1973.

Heaslip, George. *Wilt Chamberlain: A Winner.* Mankato, Minnesota: Creative Education, 1973.

Rudeen, Kenneth. *Wilt Chamberlain.* New York: Thomas Y. Crowell, 1970.

Carpenter, Harry. *Masters of Boxing.* New York: A.S. Barnes, 1964, pp. 52–65.

Heller, Peter. *In This Corner . . .! Forty World Champions Tell Their Stories.* New York: Simon and Schuster, 1973.

Marsh, Irving T., and Edward Ehre, eds. *Best Sports Stories.* ["The Longest Day of Sugar Ray," Dave Anderson, pp. 35–48]. New York: E.P. Dutton, 1965.

Baker, Jim. *Billie Jean King.* New York: Grosset & Dunlap, 1974.

King, Billie Jean, and Frank Deford. *Billie Jean.* New York: Viking Press, 1982.

King, Billie Jean, and Joe Hyams. *Billie Jean King's Secrets of Winning Tennis.* New York: Holt, Rinehart, 1974.

Baldwin, Stanley, and Jerry Jenkins with Hank Aaron. *Bad Henry.* Radnor, Pennsylvania: Chilton, 1974.

Hahn, James, and Lynn Hahn. *Henry!: The Sports Career of Henry Aaron.* Mankato, Minnesota: Crestwood House, 1981.

Hirshberg, Albert. *The Up-to-Date Biography of Henry Aaron: Quiet Superstar.* New York: G.P. Putnam, 1974.

Brown, Jim, and Steve Delsohn. *Out of Bounds.* New York: Kensington, 1989.

Hahn, James, and Lynn Hahn. *Brown!: The Sports Career of James Brown.* Mankato, Minnesota: Crestwood House, 1981.

May, Julian. *Jim Brown: Runs with the Ball.* Mankato, Minnesota, Crestwood House, 1972.

Chapter Six. Writers

Answers: 1. Nathaniel Hawthorne; 2. Ernest Hemingway; 3. John Steinbeck; 4. F. (Francis) Scott Fitzgerald; 5. Herman Melville; 6. Harriet Beecher Stowe; 7. Mark Twain; 8. Pearl S. (Sydenstricker) Buck; 9. Harry "Sinclair" Lewis; 10. William Faulkner; 11. Louisa May Alcott; 12. James Baldwin.

Turner, Arlin. *Nathaniel Hawthorne: A Biography.* New York: Oxford University Press, 1980.

Wagenknecht, Edward. *Nathaniel Hawthorne: The Man, His Tales and Romances.* New York: Continuum, 1989.

Young, Philip. *Hawthorne's Secret: An Un-told Tale.* Boston: D.R. Godine, 1984.

Baker, Carlos. *Ernest Hemingway: A Life Story.* New York: Charles Scribner's Sons, 1969.

Hemingway, Mary Welsh. *How It Was.* New York: Alfred A. Knopf, 1976.

Lynn, Kenneth S. *Hemingway.* New York: Simon and Schuster, 1987.

Benson, Jackson J. *The True Adventures of John Steinbeck, Writer.* New York: Viking Press, 1984.

Ferrell, Keith. *John Steinbeck. The Voice of the Land.* New York: M. Evans, 1986.

Steinbeck, Elaine, and Robert Wallsten, eds. *Steinbeck: A Life in Letters.* New York: Viking Press, 1975.

Buttitta, Tony. *The Lost Summer: A Personal Memoir of F. Scott Fitzgerald.* New York: St. Martin's, 1987.

Greenfeld, Howard. *F. Scott Fitzgerald.* New York: Crown, 1974.

Le Vot, Andre. *F. Scott Fitzgerald: A Biography.* Garden City, New York: Doubleday, 1983.

Allen, Gay Wilson. *Melville and His World.* New York: Viking Press, 1971.

Hillway, Tyrus. *Herman Melville.* Boston: Twayne, 1979.

Howard, Leon. *Herman Melville: A Biography.* California: University of California Press, 1981.

Ash, Maureen. *The Story of Harriet Beecher Stowe.* Chicago: Children's Press, 1990.

Gerson, Noel Bertram. *Harriet Beecher Stowe: A Biography.* New York: Popular Library, 1976.

Johnston, Johanna. *Harriet and the Runaway Book: The Story of Harriet Beecher Stowe and* Uncle Tom's Cabin. New York: Harper & Row, 1977.

Lauber, John. *The Making of Mark Twain: A Biography.* New York: American Heritage, 1985.

Meltzer, Milton. *Mark Twain. A Writer's Life.* New York: F. Watts, 1985.

Sanborn, Margaret. *Mark Twain: The Bachelor Years: A Biography.* New York: Doubleday, 1990.

Harris, Theodore F., and Pearl S. Buck. *Pearl S. Buck: A Biography.* 2 vols. New York: The John Day Company, 1969.

La Farge, Ann. *Pearl Buck.* New York: Chelsea House, 1988.

Rizzon, Beverly E. *Pearl S. Buck: The Final Chapter.* Palm Springs, California: ETC, 1989.

Dooley, David J. *The Art of Sinclair Lewis.* Lincoln, Nebraska: University of Nebraska Press, 1967.

Grebstein, Sheldon Norman. *Sinclair Lewis.* New York: Twayne, 1962.

Schorer, Mark. *Sinclair Lewis: An American Life.* New York: McGraw-Hill, 1961.

Minter, David. *William Faulkner: His Life and Work.* Baltimore, Maryland: Johns Hopkins University Press, 1982.

Oates, Stephen B. *William Faulkner: The Man and the Artist.* New York: Harper & Row, 1987.

Putzee, Max. *Genius of Place: William Faulkner's Triumphant Beginnings.* Baton Rouge, Louisiana: Louisiana State University Press, 1985.

Burke, Kathleen. *Louisa May Alcott.* New York: Chelsea House, 1988.

Myerson, Joel, and Daniel Shealy, eds. *The Journals of Louisa May Alcott.* Boston: Little, Brown, 1989.

Saxton, Martha. *Louisa May: A Modern Biography of Louisa May Alcott.* New York: Houghton Mifflin, 1977.

Rosset, Lisa. *James Baldwin.* New York: Chelsea House, 1989.

Troupe, Quincy, ed. *James Baldwin: The Legacy.* New York: Simon and Schuster, 1989.

Weatherby, William J. *James Baldwin: Artist on Fire: A Portrait.* New York: D.I. Fine, 1989.

Chapter Seven. Inventors

Answers: 1. Eli Whitney; 2. Thomas Alva Edison; 3. Charles Goodyear; 4. Robert Fulton; 5. Henry Ford; 6. Luther Burbank; 7. Wilbur and Orville

Wright; 8. George Eastman; 9. Samuel Colt; 10. Benjamin Franklin; 11. Elias Howe; 12. John Deere.

Hays, Wilma Pitchford. *Eli Whitney. Founder of Modern Industry.* New York: F. Watts, 1965.

Howard, Robert West. *Eli Whitney.* Chicago: Follett, 1966.

Olmsted, Dennison. *Memoir of Eli Whitney, Esq.* New York: Arno Press, 1972.

Egan, Louise. *Thomas Edison, The Great American Inventor.* Chicago, Illinois: Children's Press Choice, 1988.

Friedel, Robert D., Paul Israel, and Bernard S. Finn. *Edison's Electric Light: Biography of an Inventor.* New Brunswick, New Jersey: Rutgers University Press, 1986.

Millard, Andre. *Edison and the Business of Innovation.* Baltimore: Johns Hopkins University Press, 1990.

Barker, Preston Wallace. *Charles Goodyear: Connecticut Yankee and Rubber Pioneer: A Biography.* Boston: G.L. Cabot, 1940.

Quackenbush, Robert M. *Oh, What an Awful Mess!: A Story of Charles Goodyear.* Englewood Cliffs, New Jersey: Prentice-Hall, 1980.

Regli, Adolph C. *Rubber's Goodyear: The Story of Man's Perseverance.* New York: J. Messner, 1941.

Henry, Joanne Landers. *Robert Fulton. Steamboat Builder.* New York: Chelsea Juniors, 1991.

Philip, Cynthia Owen. *Robert Fulton: A Biography.* New York: F. Watts, 1985.

Radford, Ruby Lorraine. *Robert Fulton.* New York: Putnam, 1970.

Bryan, Ford Richardson. *Beyond the Model T: The Other Ventures of Henry Ford.* Detroit: Wayne State University Press, 1990.

Bryan, Ford Richardson. *The Fords of Dearborn.* Detroit, Michigan: Harlo, 1987.

Lacey, Robert. *Ford: The Man and the Machine.* Boston: Little, Brown, 1986.

Dreyer, Peter. *A Gardener Touched with Genius: The Life of Luther Burbank.* Berkeley: University of California Press, 1985.

Kraft, Ken, and Pat Kraft. *Luther Burbank: The Wizard and the Man.* New York: Meredith Press, 1967.

Quackenbush, Robert M. *Here a Plant, There a Plant, Everywhere a Plant!: A Story of Luther Burbank.* Englewood Cliffs, New Jersey: Prentice-Hall, 1982.

Crouch, Tom D. *The Bishop's Boys: A Life of the Wright Brothers.* New York: W.W. Norton, 1989.

Howard, Fred. *Wilbur and Orville: A Biography of the Wright Brothers.* New York: Knopf, 1987.

Taylor, Richard L. *The First Flight: The Story of the Wright Brothers.* New York: F. Watts, 1990.

Ackerman, Carl William. *George Eastman.* New York: Houghton Mifflin, 1930.

Henry, Joanne Landers. *George Eastman, Young Photographer.* Indianapolis: Bobbs-Merrill, 1959.

Mitchell, Barbara. *Click! A Story About George Eastman.* Minneapolis: Carolrhonda Books, 1986.

Haven, Charles T., and Frank A. Belden. *A History of the Colt Revolver, and the Other Arms Made by Colt's Patent Fire Arms Manufacturing Company from 1836 to 1940.* New York: W. Morrow, 1940.

Keating, Bern. *The Flamboyant Mr. Colt and His Deadly Six-Shooter.* Garden City, New York: Doubleday, 1978.

Winders, Gertrude Hecker. *Sam Colt and His Gun: The Life of the Inventor of the Revolver.* New York: Jay Day, 1959.

Franklin, Benjamin. *The Autobiography of Benjamin Franklin.* New York: Buccaneer, 1984.

Franklin, Benjamin, and Kenneth Silverman. *Autobiography and Other Writings.* New York: Penguin Books, 1986.

Wright, Esmond, ed. *Benjamin Franklin: His Life as He Wrote It.* Cambridge, Massachusetts: Harvard University Press, 1990.

Corcoran, Jean. *Elias Howe. Inventive Boy.* Indianapolis: Bobbs-Merrill, 1962.

Feldman, Anthony, and Peter Ford. *Scientists and Inventors.* New York: Facts on File, 1979, pp. 154–155.

The National Cyclopaedia of American Biography. vol. IV. New York: James T. White & Company, 1897, pp. 432–433.

Bare, Margaret Ann. *John Deere, Blacksmith Boy.* Indianapolis: Bobbs-Merrill, 1964.

Broehl, Wayne G. *John Deere's Company: A History of Deere & Company and Its Times.* New York: Doubleday, 1984.

Clark, Neil McCullough. *John Deere: He Gave to the World the Steel Plow.* Moline, Illinois: Desaulniers, 1937.

Chapter Eight. Musicians/Composers

Answers: 1. Cole Porter; 2. Leonard Bernstein; 3. Oscar Hammerstein II; 4. George Gershwin; 5. Stephen Collins Foster; 6. George M. (Michael) Cohan; 7. W.C. (William Christopher) Handy; 8. John Philip Sousa; 9. Meredith Willson; 10. Alan Jay Lerner; 11. Woody Guthrie; 12. Aaron Copland.

Eells, George. *The Life That Late He Led: A Biography of Cole Porter.* New York: G.P. Putnam's Sons, 1967.

Kimball, Robert, and Brendan Gill, eds. *Cole.* New York: Holt, Rinehart & Winston, 1971.

Schwartz, Charles. *Cole Porter: A Biography.* New York: Dial, 1977.

Gradenwitz, Peter. *Leonard Bernstein: The Infinite Variety of a Musician.* New York: Berg, 1987.

Peyser, Joan. *Bernstein, A Biography.* New York: Beech Tree, 1987.

Robinson, Paul. *Bernstein.* New York: Vanguard, 1982.

Fordin, Hugh. *Getting to Know Him: A Biography of Oscar Hammerstein II.* New York: Random House, 1986.

Nolan, Frederick W. *The Sound of Their Music: The Story of Rodgers & Hammerstein.* New York: Walker, 1978.

Taylor, Deems. *Some Enchanted Evenings: The Story of Rodgers and Hammerstein.* New York: Harper, 1953.

Jablonski, Edward. *Gershwin.* New York: Doubleday, 1987.

Kendall, Alan. *George Gershwin: A Biography.* New York: Universe, 1987.

Mitchell, Barbara. *America. I Hear You: A Story About George Gershwin.* Minneapolis: Carolrhoda, 1987.

Hodges, Fletcher. *Swanee Ribber and a Biographical Sketch of Stephen Collins Foster.* White Springs, Florida: Stephen Foster Memorial Association, 1958.

Howard, John Tasker. *Stephen Foster, America's Troubadour.* New York: T.Y. Crowell, 1962.

Howard, John Tasker. *A Treasury of Stephen Foster.* New York: Random House, 1946.

Cohan, George M. *Twenty Years on Broadway and the Years It Took to Get There; The True Story of a Trouper's Life from the Cradle to the "Closed Shop."* New York: Harper & Brothers, 1925.

McCabe, John. *George M. Cohan. The Man Who Owned Broadway.* New York: Da Capo, 1980.

Morehouse, Ward. *George M. Cohan: Prince of the American Theater.* New York: J.B. Lippincott, 1943.

Bontemps, Arna, ed. *Father of the Blues: An Autobiography.* New York: Collier, 1970.

Montgomery, Elizabeth Rider. *William C. Handy: Father of the Blues.* Champaign, Illinois: Garrard, 1968.

Wayne, Bennett. *3 Jazz Greats.* Champaign, Illinois: Garrard, 1973.

Bierley, Paul E. *John Philip Sousa: American Phenomenon.* New York: Appleton-Century-Crofts, 1973.

Bierley, Paul E. *John Philip Sousa: A Descriptive Catalog of His Works.* Urbana, Illinois: University of Illinois Press, 1973.

Bierley, Paul E. *The Works of John Philip Sousa.* Columbus, Ohio: Integrity, 1984.

Hitchcock, H. Wiley, ed. *The New Grove Dictionary of American Music.* vol. 4. New York: Grove's, 1986, p. 537.

Willson, Meredith. *The Music Man.* Boston: Frank Music Corp. and Rinimer Corporation, 1957.

Willson, Meredith. *There I Stood with My Piccolo.* New York: Doubleday, 1948.

Leos, Gene. *Inventing Champagne: The Worlds of Lerner and Loewe.* New York: St. Martin's, 1990.

Lerner, Alan Jay. *The Street Where I Live: The Story of* My Fair Lady, Gigi *and* Camelot. London: Columbus, 1989.

Shapiro, Doris. *We Danced All Night: My Life Behind the Scenes with Alan Jay Lerner.* New York: Morrow, 1990.

Guthrie, Woody. *Bound for Glory.* New York: E.P. Dutton, 1976.

Guthrie, Woody, Dave Marsh, and Harold Leventhal, eds. *Pastures of Plenty: A Self-Portrait.* New York: Harper-Collins, 1990.

Klein, Joe. *Woody Guthrie: A Life.* New York: A.A. Knopf, 1980.
Copland, Aaron, and Vivian Perlis. *Copland: Since 1943.* New York: St. Martin's, 1989.
Skowronski, JoAnn. *Aaron Copland, A Bio-Bibliography.* Westport, Connecticut: Greenwood, 1985.
Smith, Julia Frances. *Aaron Copland. His Work and Contribution to American Music.* New York: Dutton, 1955.

Chapter Nine. Folk Heroes

Answers: 1. Johnny Appleseed; 2. Billy the Kid; 3. David "Davy" Crockett; 4. Jesse Woodson James; 5. Daniel Boone; 6. Calamity Jane; 7. John Henry; 8. Annie Oakley; 9. John Luther "Casey" Jones; 10. Uncle Remus; 11. Pecos Bill; 12. Paul Bunyan.

Kellogg, Steven. *Johnny Appleseed.* New York: Morrow Junior, 1988.
Kellogg, Steven. *Johnny Appleseed: A Tall Tale.* New York: Morrow Junior, 1988.
Nissenson, Hugh. *The Tree of Life.* New York: Harper & Row, 1985.
Garrett, Patrick Floyd. *The Authentic Life of Billy the Kid.* Norman, Oklahoma: University of Oklahoma Press, 1986.
McMurtry, Larry. *Anything for Billy.* New York: Simon & Schuster, 1988.
Momaday, N. Scott. *The Ancient Child: A Novel.* New York: Doubleday, 1989.
Facsim, A., ed., James S. Shackford, and Stanley J. Folmsbee. *A Narrative of the Life of David Crockett of the State of Tennessee.* Knoxville: University of Tennessee Press, 1973.
Lofaro, Michael A. *Davy Crockett: The Man, the Legend, the Legacy, 1786–1986.* Knoxville: University of Tennessee Press, 1985.
Parks, Aileen Wells. *Davy Crockett: Young Rifleman.* Indianapolis: Bobbs-Merrill, 1983.
Baldwin, Margaret, and Pat O'Brien. *Wanted, Frank & James: The Real Story.* New York: J. Messner, 1981.
Love, Robertus. *The Rise and Fall of Jesse James.* Lincoln: University of Nebraska Press, 1990.
Snell, Joseph. *The Life, Times, and Treacherous Death of Jesse James.* Chicago: Swallow, 1970.
Lofaro, Michael A. *The Life and Adventures of Daniel Boone.* Lexington: University Press of Kentucky, 1986.
May, Robin. *Daniel Boone and the American West.* New York: Bookwright, 1986.
Zadra, Dan. *Daniel Boone: In the Wilderness 1734–1820.* Mankato, Minnesota: Creative Education, 1988.
The Encyclopedia Americana. International ed. vol. 5. Danbury, Connecticut: Grolier, 1991, p. 156.
McMurtry, Larry. *Buffalo Girls: A Novel.* New York: Simon and Schuster, 1990.

The New Encyclopaedia Britannica. 15th ed. vol. 2. Chicago: Encyclopaedia Britannica, 1986, pp. 731–732.

Felton, Harold W. *John Henry and His Hammer.* New York: Knopf, 1950.

Sanfield, Steve. *A Natural Man: The True Story of John Henry.* Boston: D.R. Godine, 1986.

Williams, Brett. *John Henry, A Bio-Bibliography.* Westport, Connecticut: Greenwood, 1983.

Alderman, Clifford Lindsey. *Annie Oakley and the World of Her Time.* New York: Macmillan, 1979.

Sayers, Isabelle S. *Annie Oakley and Buffalo Bill's Wild West.* New York: Dover, 1981.

Quackenbush, Robert M. *Who's That Girl with the Gun?: A Story of Annie Oakley.* New York: Prentice-Hall Books for Young Readers, 1988.

Lee, Fred J. *Casey Jones: Epic of the American Railroad.* Kingsport, Tennessee: Southern, 1939.

Rounds, Glen. *Casey Jones: The Story of a Brave Engineer.* San Carlos, California: Golden Gated Junior Books, 1968.

York, Carol Beach, and Bert Dodson. *Casey Jones.* Mahwah, New Jersey: Troll, 1980.

Baer, Florence E. *Sources and Analogues of the Uncle Remus Tales.* Helsinki: Suomalainen Tiedeakatemia, 1980.

Harris, Joel Chandler. *Uncle Remus. His Songs and His Sayings.* Norwood, Pennsylvania: Telegraph, 1985.

Harris, Joel Chandler, and Richard Chase. *The Complete Tales of Uncle Remus.* Boston: Houghton Mifflin, 1955.

Bowman, James Cloyd. *Pecos Bill. The Greatest Cowboy of All Time.* Chicago: A. Whitman, 1937.

Felton, Harold W. *New Tall Tales of Pecos Bill.* Englewood Cliffs, New Jersey: Prentice-Hall, 1958.

Kellogg, Steven. *Pecos Bill: A Tall Tale.* New York: Morrow, 1986.

Felton, Harold W., ed. *Legends of Paul Bunyan.* New York: A.A. Knopf, 1947.

Lewis, Allen. *Paul Bunyan: Woodcuts.* New York: A.A. Knopf, 1948.

Stevens, James. *The Saginaw Paul Bunyan.* Detroit: Wayne State University Press, 1987.

Chapter Ten. *Merchants/Entrepreneurs*

Answers: 1. J.C. (James Cash) Penney; 2. Ray Kroc; 3. Frank Winfield Woolworth; 4. Harland Sanders; 5. Richard W. (Warren) Sears; 6. Mary Kay Ash; 7. Burton Baskin; 8. Aaron Montgomery Ward; 9. Wally Amos; 10. Sebastian S. (Spering) Kresge; 11. Samuel "Sam" Moore Walton; 12. Debbie Fields.

Beasley, Norman. *Main Street Merchant: The Story of the J.C. Penney Company.* New York: Whittlesey House, 1948.

Bruere, Robert W., and J.C. Penney. *J.C. Penney: The Man with a Thousand Partners: An Autobiography of J.C. Penney.* New York: Harper & Brothers, 1931.

Plumb, Beatrice. *J.C. Penney. Merchant Prince: A Biography of a Man Who Built a Business Empire Based on the Golden Rule.* Minneapolis: T.S. Denison, 1963.

Boas, Maxwell. *Big Mac: The Unauthorized Story of McDonald's.* New York: New American Library, 1977.

Kroc, Ray, and Robert Anderson. *Grinding It Out: The Making of McDonald's.* Chicago: H. Regnery, 1977.

Love, John F. *McDonald's: Behind the Arches.* New York: Bantam, 1986.

Baker, Nina Brown. *Nickels and Dimes: The Story of F.W. Woolworth.* New York: Harcourt, Brace, 1954.

Winkler, John Kennedy. *Five and Ten; The Fabulous Life of F.W. Woolworth.* New York: R.M. McBride, 1940.

Woolworth Company, F.W. *Woolworth's First 75 Years; The Story of Everybody's Store.* New York: F.W. Woolworth, 1954.

Moritz, Charles, ed. *Current Biography Yearbook 1973.* New York: H.W. Wilson, 1973, pp. 374–376.

Pearce, John Ed. *The Colonel: The Captivating Biography of the Dynamic Founder of a Fast-Food Empire.* Garden City, New York: Doubleday, 1982.

Sanders, Harland. *Life as I Have Known It Has Been Finger Lickin' Good.* Carol Stream, Illinois: Creation House, 1974.

Asher, Louis E., and Edith Heal. *Send No Money.* Chicago: Argus, 1942.

Blum, Stella, ed. *Everyday Fashions of the Thirties as Pictured in Sears Catalogs.* New York: Dover, 1986.

Malone, Dumas, ed. *Dictionary of American Biography* vol. 8. New York: Charles Scribner's Sons, 1935.

Ash, Mary Kay. *Mary Kay.* New York: Harper & Row, 1986.

Fucini, Joseph J., and Suzy Fucini. *Entrepreneurs: The Men and Women Behind Famous Brand Names and How They Made It.* Boston: G.K. Hall, 1985, pp. 96–99.

NyKoruk, Barbara, ed. *Business People in the News.* vol. 1. Detroit: Gale Research, 1976.

Fucini, Joseph J., and Suzy Fucini. *Entrepreneurs: The Men and Women Behind Famous Brand Names and How They Made It.* Boston: G.K. Hall, 1985, pp. 32–34.

O'Roark, Mary Ann. *The Baskin-Robbins Book of Ice Cream, Entertaining and Fun.* New York: Simon and Schuster, 1980.

"When Your Image Is Frozen in Time." *Working Woman,* October 1990, pp. 53–54.

Baker, Nina Brown. *Big Catalogue: The Life of Aaron Montgomery Ward.* New York: Harcourt, 1956.

Johnson, Allen, and Dumas Malone, eds. *Dictionary of American Biography.* 20 vols. 7 suppls. New York: Charles Scribner's Sons, 1958.

The National Cyclopaedia of American Biography. 13 vols. Ann Arbor, Michigan: University Microfilms, 1967, p. 38.

Amos, Wally. "Famous Amos' Dynamite Double-Chocolate Desserts." *Redbook*, February 1989, pp. 111–114.

Amos, Wally, and Leroy Robinson. *The Famous Amos Story: The Face That Launched a Thousand Chips*. Garden City, New York: Doubleday & Company, Inc., 1983.

"Famous Amos Sells His Popular Cookie Company," *Jet*, May 23, 1988, p. 16.

Kresge, S.S. Company. *Kresge's Katalog of 5¢ and 10¢ Merchandise*. New York: Random House, 1975.

Kresge, Stanley S., and Steve Spilos. *The S.S. Kresge Story*. Racine, Wisconsin: Western, 1979.

The National Cyclopedia of American Biography. 52 vols. New York: James T. White, 1970, pp. 346–347.

Barrier, Michael. "Walton's Mountain." *Nation's Business*, April 1988, pp. 18–23.

Castro, Janet. "Mr. Sam Stuns Goliath: After a Century as the Giant of U.S. Retailing, Sears Loses the Top Spot to Folksy, Hard-Charging Wal-Mart." *Time*, February 25, 1991, pp. 62–63.

Trimble, Vance H. *Sam Walton: The Inside Story of America's Richest Man*. New York: Dutton, 1990.

Conlin, Elizabeth. "The Great Giveaway." *Inc.*, May 1990, p. 27.

Fields, Debbi, and Alan Furst. *One Smart Cookie: How a Housewife's Chocolate Chip Recipe Turned Into a Multi-million Dollar Business — The Story of Mrs. Field's Cookies*. New York: Simon and Schuster, 1987.

Weisman, Katherine. "Succeeding by Failing." *Forbes*, June 25, 1990, p. 160.

Chapter Eleven. Artists

Answers: 1. Norman Rockwell; 2. Anna Mary Robertson "Grandma Moses"; 3. Andy Warhol; 4. Georgia O'Keeffe; 5. Andrew Newell Wyeth; 6. Benjamin West; 7. Gilbert Stuart; 8. Grant Wood; 9. Nathaniel Currier; 10. Mary Cassatt; 11. Charles Marion Russell; 12. Winslow Homer.

Finch, Christopher. *Norman Rockwell*. New York: Abbeville, 1980.

Rockwell, Norman, and Thomas Rockwell. *My Adventures as an Illustrator*. New York: Abrams, 1988.

Walton, Donald. *A Rockwell Portrait: An Intimate Biography*. Kansas City: Sheed Andrews and McMeel, 1978.

Armstrong, William Howard. *Barefoot in the Grass: The Story of Grandma Moses*. Garden City, New York: Doubleday, 1970.

Biracree, Tom. *Grandma Moses*. New York: Chelsea House, 1989.

Kallir, Otto, ed. *Art and Life of Grandma Moses*. New York: A.S. Barnes, 1969.

Bockris, Victor. *The Life and Death of Andy Warhol*. New York: Bantam, 1989.

Bourdon, David. *Warhol*. New York: H.N. Abrams, 1989.

Colacello, Bob. *Holy Terror: Andy Warhol Close Up*. New York: HarperCollins, 1990.

Castro, Jan Garden. *The Art and Life of Georgia O'Keeffe.* New York: Crown, 1985.

O'Keeffe, Georgia. *Georgia O'Keeffe.* New York: Viking Press, 1976.

Robinson, Roxana. *Georgia O'Keeffe: A Life.* New York: Harper & Row, 1989.

Corn, Wanda M. *The Art of Andrew Wyeth.* Greenwich, Connecticut: New York Graphic Society, 1973.

Logsdon, Gene. *Wyeth People: A Portrait of Andrew Wyeth as He Is Seen by His Friends and Neighbors.* Garden City: New York: Doubleday, 1971.

Meryman, Richard. *Andrew Wyeth.* Boston: Houghton Mifflin, 1968.

Abrams, Ann Uhry. *The Valiant Hero: Benjamin West and Grand-Style History Painting.* Washington, DC: Smithsonian Institution, 1985.

Alberts, Robert C. *Benjamin West: A Biography.* Boston: Houghton Mifflin, 1978.

Kraemer, Ruth S. *Drawings by Benjamin West and His Son Raphael Lamar West.* New York: Pierpont Morgan Library, 1975.

McLanathan, Richard. *Gilbert Stuart.* New York: Abrams, 1986.

Merrill, Charles. *Gilbert Stuart: A Biography.* New York: W.W. Norton, 1964.

Whitley, William Thomas. *Gilbert Stuart.* Cambridge, Massachusetts: Harvard University Press, 1932.

Dennis, James M. *Grant Wood: A Study in American Art and Culture.* Columbia: University of Missouri Press, 1986.

Goldstein, Ernest. *Grant Wood: American Gothic.* Champaign, Illinois: Garrard, 1984.

Liffring-Zug, Joan, and John Zug. *This Is Grant Wood Country.* Davenport, Iowa: Davenport Municipal Art Gallery, 1977.

Baragwanath, A.K. *100 Currier & Ives Favorites.* New York: Crown, 1978.

Crouse, Russell. *Mr. Currier and Mr. Ives. A Note on Their Lives and Times.* Garden City, New York: Doubleday, 1941.

King, Roy, and Burke Davis. *The World of Currier & Ives.* New York: Random House, 1968.

Cain, Michael. *Mary Cassatt.* New York: Chelsea House, 1989.

Coe, Kerr Gallery. *Mary Cassatt. An American Observer: A Loan Exhibition for the Benefit of the American Wing of the Metropolitan Museum of Art (October 3rd to 27th, 1984).* New York: The Gallery, 1984.

Getlein, Frank. *Mary Cassatt: Paintings and Prints.* New York: Abbeville, 1980.

Aldrich, Lanning, ed. *The Western Art of Charles M. Russell.* New York: Ballantine, 1975.

Gale, Robert L. *Charles Marion Russell.* Boise, Idaho: Boise State University Press, 1979.

Hassrick, Peter H. *Charles M. Russell.* New York: Abrams, 1989.

Cikovsky, Nicolai, Jr. *Winslow Homer.* New York: Abrams, 1990.

Hendricks, Gordon. *The Life and Work of Winslow Homer.* New York: H.N. Abrams, 1979.

Hyman, Linda. *Winslow Homer: America's Old Master.* Garden City, New York: Doubleday, 1973.

Chapter Twelve. Heroes of the Olympic Games

Answers: 1. Wilma Rudolph; 2. George Foreman; 3. Peggy Fleming; 4. Jim Thorpe; 5. Jesse Owens; 6. Mary Lou Retton; 7. Greg Louganis; 8. Carl Lewis; 9. Mark Spitz; 10. Robert "Bob" Beamon; 11. Rafer Johnson; 12. Deborah "Debbie" Meyer.

Berke, Art, and William Redding, eds. *The Lincoln Library of Sports Champions.* 14 vols. Columbus, Ohio: Sports Resources Company, 1974, pp. 68–71 (vol. 2).

Biracree, Tom. *Wilma Rudolph.* New York: Chelsea House, 1988.

Jacobs, Linda. *Wilma Rudolph: Run for Glory.* St. Paul, Minnesota: EMC, 1975.

Berke, Art, and William Redding, eds. *The Lincoln Library of Sports Champions.* 14 vols. Columbus, Ohio: Sports Resources Company, 1974, pp. 158–165 (vol. 4).

Gardner, Leonard. "Pain and Violence as a Way of Life." *Best Sports Stories.* Eds. Irving T. Marsh and Edward Ehre. New York: E.P. Dutton, 1973. pp. 168– 182.

Muller, Eddie. "It Took Him 45 Minutes 35 Seconds." *Best Sports Stories.* Eds. Irving T. Marsh and Edward Ehre, New York: E.P. Dutton, 1973. pp. 172– 176.

Berke, Art and William Redding, eds. *The Lincoln Library of Sports Champions.* 14 vols. Columbus, Ohio: Sports Resources Company, 1974, pp. 142–147 (vol. 4).

Morse, Charles, and Ann Morse. *Peggy Fleming.* Mankato, Minnesota: Creative Education, 1974.

Van Steenwyk, Elizabeth. *Peggy Fleming: Cameo of a Champion.* New York: McGraw-Hill, 1978.

Hahn, James, and Lynn Hahn. *Thorpe! The Sports Career of James Thorpe.* Mankato, Minnesota: Crestwood House, 1981.

Richards, Gregory B. *Jim Thorpe, World's Greatest Athlete.* Chicago: Children's Press, 1984.

Schoor, Gene, and Henry Gilfond. *The Jim Thorpe Story, America's Greatest Athlete.* New York: Messner, 1951.

Baker, William Joseph. *Jesse Owens, An American Life.* New York: Free Press, 1986.

Owens, Jesse, and Paul Neimark. *Jesse, A Spiritual Autobiography.* Plainfield, New Jersey: Logos International, 1978.

Sabin, Francene. *Jesse Owens, Olympic Hero.* Mahwah, New Jersey: Troll, 1986.

Retton, Mary Lou, Bela Karolyi and John Powers. *Mary Lou Retton: Creating an Olympic Champion.* New York: McGraw-Hill, 1986.

Silverstein, Herman. *Mary Lou Retton and the New Gymnasts.* New York: F. Watts, 1985.

Sullivan, George. *Mary Lou Retton: A Biography.* New York: Julian Messner, 1985.

"The Legacy of Greg Louganis." *Sports Illustrated*, September 14, 1988, pp. 86–87.

Michelmore, Peter. "Greg Louganis: High Diver with Heart." *Reader's Digest*, June 1988, pp. 163–167.

Milton, Joyce. *Greg Louganis: Diving for Gold*. New York: Random House, 1989.

Aaseng, Nathan. *Carl Lewis: Legend Chaser*. Minneapolis: Lerner, 1985.

Lewis, Carl, and Jeffrey Marx. *Inside Track: My Professional Life in Amateur Track*. New York: Simon and Schuster, 1990.

Rosenthal, Bert. *Carl Lewis, The Second Jesse Owens*. Chicago: Children's Press, 1984.

Berke, Art, and William Redding, eds. *The Lincoln Library of Sports Champions*. 14 vols. Columbus, Ohio: Sports Resources Company, 1974, pp. 66–73 (vol. 12).

Olsen, James T. *Mark Spitz: The Shark*. Mankato, Minnesota: Creative Education, 1974.

Taylor, Paula. *Mark Spitz*. Mankato, Minnesota: Creative Education, 1976.

Berke, Art, and William Redding, eds. *The Lincoln Library of Sports Champions*. 14 vols. Columbus, Ohio: Sports Resources Company, 1974, pp. 180–185 (vol. 1).

McCallum, Jack. "The Record Company." *Sports Illustrated*, January 8, 1990, p. 58.

Moore, Kenny. "Giants on the Earth." *Sports Illustrated*, June 29, 1987, p. 48.

Berke, Art, and William Redding, eds. *The Lincoln Library of Sports Champions*. 14 vols. Columbus, Ohio: Sports Resources Company, 1974, pp. 182–187 (vol. 6).

Phillips, Bob. "Still Carrying the Torch." *Scholastic Coach*, August 1988, pp. 38–42.

Schwartz, Bert. *Great Black Athletes*. West Haven, Connecticut: Pendulum, 1971.

Berke, Art, and William Redding, eds. *The Lincoln Library of Sports Champions*. 14 vols. Columbus, Ohio: Sports Resources Company, 1974, pp. 48–51 (vol. 9).

Besford, Pat, ed. *Encyclopaedia of Swimming*. 2nd ed. New York: St. Martin's, 1976.

Moritz, Charles. *Current Biography Yearbook 1969*. New York: The H.W. Wilson Company, 1969, pp. 289–291.

Bibliography

Abbott, David, Ph.D., ed. *The Biographical Dictionary of Scientists, Engineers and Inventors.* New York: Peter Bedrick, 1985.

Academic American Encyclopedia. 21 vols. Danbury, Connecticut: Grolier, 1986.

Affron, Charles. *Star Acting: Gish, Garbo, Davis.* New York: E.P. Dutton, 1977.

Amos, Wally, and Leroy Robinson. *The Famous Amos Story: The Face That Launched a Thousand Chips.* Garden City, New York: Doubleday, 1983.

Baragwanath, A.K. *100 Currier & Ives Favorites.* New York: Crown, 1978.

Bawden, Liz-Anne, ed. *The Oxford Companion to Film.* New York: Oxford University Press, 1976.

Berke, Art, and William Redding, eds. *The Lincoln Library of Sports Champions.* 14 vols. Columbus, Ohio: Sports Resources Company, 1974.

Bierley, Paul E. *John Philip Sousa: A Descriptive Catalog of His Works.* Urbana, Chicago: University of Illinois Press, 1973.

Boller, Paul F., Jr. *Presidential Wives: An Anecdotal History.* New York: Oxford University Press, 1988.

Blum, John M., et al., eds. *The National Experience: A History of the United States to 1877, Part One.* New York: Harcourt Brace Jovanovich, 1977.

Cohen, Daniel, and Susan Cohen. *Hollywood Hunks and Heroes.* New York: Exeter, 1985.

Courthion, Pierre, and John Shepley. *Impressionism.* New York: Harry N. Abrams, 1977.

Davis, Lenwood G., and Belinda S. Daniels. *Black Athletes in the United States: A Bibliography of Books, Articles, Autobiographies, and Biographies on Black Professional Athletes in the U.S., 1800–1981.* Westport, Connecticut: Greenwood, 1981.

Douglas, Emily Taft. *Remember the Ladies: The Story of Great Women Who Helped Shape America.* New York: G.P. Putnam's Sons, 1966.

Eliot, Alexander. *Three Hundred Years of American Painting.* New York: Time, 1957.

The Encyclopedia Americana. International Edition. 30 vols. Danbury, Connecticut: Grolier, 1989.

Ewen, David, ed. *American Popular Songs: From the Revolutionary War to the Present.* New York: Random House, 1966.

Fielding, Mantle, and Genevieve C. Doran. *Dictionary of American Painters, Sculptors and Engravers.* Green Farms, Connecticut: Modern Books and Crafts, Inc., 1974.

Fields, Debbie, and Alan Furst. *One Smart Cookie: How a Housewife's Chocolate Chip Recipe Turned Into a Multi-million Dollar Business — The Story of Mrs. Field's Cookies.* New York: Simon and Schuster, 1987.

Finch, Christopher. *Norman Rockwell's America.* Reader's Digest Edition. New York: Harry N. Abrams, 1976.

Fucini, Joseph J., and Suzy Fucini. *Entrepreneurs: The Men and Women Behind Famous Brand Names and How They Made It.* Boston: G.K. Hall, 1985.

Greenberg, Stan. *Guinness Olympic Games: The Records.* New York: Guinness Superlatives, 1987.

Grolier Encyclopedia. 20 vols. New York: The Grolier Society Publishers, 1958.

Guthrie, Woody, and Pete Seeger. *Woody Guthrie Folk Songs: A Collection of Songs by America's Foremost Balladeer.* New York: Ludlow Music, 1963.

Halliwell, Leslie. *Halliwell's Film Guide.* 7th ed. New York: Harper & Row, 1989.

Harris, Joel Chandler, and Richard Chase. *The Complete Tales of Uncle Remus.* Boston: Houghton Mifflin, 1955.

Hoffman, Mark S., ed. *The World Almanac and Book of Facts 1989.* New York: World Almanac, 1988.

James, Edward T., ed. *Notable American Women: A Biographical Dictionary.* 3 vols. Cambridge, Massachusetts: The Belknap Press of Harvard University Press, 1975.

Johnson, Allen, and Dumas Malone, eds. *Dictionary of American Biography.* 20 vols. 7 suppls. New York: Charles Scribner's Sons, 1958.

Keller, Helen. *The Story of My Life.* New York: New American Library, 1988.

The Life Treasury of American Folklore. New York: Life, Time Incorporated, 1961.

Litz, A. Walton, ed. *American Writers: A Collection of Literary Biographies.* 4 vols. 2 suppls. New York: Charles Scribner's Sons, 1981.

Loomis, Vincent, and Jeffrey Ethell. *Amelia Earhart: The Final Story.* New York: Random House, 1985.

Lovell, Mary S. *The Sound of Wings: The Life of Amelia Earhart.* New York: St. Martin's, 1989.

Lutz, Alma. *Susan B. Anthony: Rebel, Crusader, Humanitarian.* Washington, DC: Zenger Publishing, 1976.

Magill, Frank N., ed. *Great Lives from History: American Series.* 16 vols. Pasadena, California: Salem, 1987.

Maltin, Leonard, ed. *Leonard Maltin's TV Movies and Video Guide.* 1991 ed. New York: American Library, 1990.

Merriam, Eve, ed. *Growing Up Female in America: Ten Lives.* Garden City, New York: Doubleday, 1971.

Meyer, Michael, ed. *Frederick Douglass: The Narrative and Selected Writings.* New York: The Modern Library, 1984.

Miers, Earl Schenck. *America and Its Presidents.* New York: Grosset & Dunlap, 1982.

Moritz, Charles, ed. *Current Biography Yearbook.* (1940–1945, 1947, 1949, 1950–1952, 1955–1959, 1960–1964, 1967–1969, 1971–1974, 1977, 1978, 1981–1984). New York: The H.W. Wilson Company, 1991.

The National Cyclopedia of American Biography. 63 vols. New York: James T. White, 1970.

The New Encyclopaedia Britannica. 30 vols. Chicago: Encyclopaedia Britannica, 1986.

Petry, Ann. *Harriet Tubman: Conductor on the Underground Railroad.* New York: Thomas Y. Crowell, 1955.

Petteys, Chris. *Dictionary of Women Artists: An International Dictionary of Women Artists Born Before 1900.* Boston: G.K. Hall, 1985.

Ploski, Harry A., Ph.D., ed. *Reference Library of Black America.* 5 vols. New York: Bellwether, Inc., 1971.

Reader's Digest. *American Folklore and Legend.* Pleasantville, New York: The Reader's Digest, 1978.

Reader's Digest. *The Story of America.* Pleasantville, New York: The Reader's Digest, 1975.

Reichler, Joseph L. ed. *The Baseball Encyclopedia: The Complete and Official Record of Major League Baseball.* 5th ed. New York: Macmillan, 1982.

Retton, Mary Lou, Bela Karolyi, and John Powers. *Mary Lou Retton: Creating an Olympic Champion.* New York: McGraw-Hill, 1986.

Richardson, Ben, and William Fahey. *Great Black Americans.* New York: Thomas Y. Crowell, 1976.

Sadie, Stanley, ed. *The New Grove Dictionary of Music and Musicians.* 20 vols. Washington, DC: Grove's Dictionaries of Music, 1981.

Sobel, Robert, and David B. Sicilia. *The Entrepreneurs: An American Adventure.* Boston: Houghton Mifflin, 1986.

Spada, James. *Grace: The Secret Lives of a Princess.* Garden City, New York: Doubleday, 1987.

Sparhawk, Ruth M., Mary E. Leslie, Phyllis Y. Turbow, and Zina R. Rose, eds. *American Women in Sport. 1887–1987. A 100-Year Chronology.* Metuchen, New Jersey: The Scarecrow Press, Inc., 1989.

Stetler, Susan L., ed. *Almanac of Famous People.* 4th ed. 3 vols. Detroit: Gale Research, 1989.

Trimble, Vance H. *Sam Walton: The Inside Story of America's Richest Man.* New York: A Dutton Book/Penguin Books, 1990.

Unger, Leonard, ed. *American Writers: A Collection of Literary Biographies.* 4 vols. 4 suppls. New York: Charles Scribner's Sons, 1974.

Van Doren, Charles Lincoln, ed. *Webster's American Biographies.* Springfield, Massachusetts: G. & C. Merriam, 1974.

Wagenknecht, Edward. *Harriet Beecher Stowe: The Known and the Unknown.* New York: Oxford University Press, 1965.

Wallechinsky, David. *The Complete Book of the Olympics.* New York: Penguin, 1988.

Whitman, Alden, ed. *American Reformers: An H.W. Wilson Biographical Dictionary.* New York: The H.W. Wilson Company, 1985.

Willson, Meredith. *The Music Man.* Boston: Frank Music Corp. and Rinimer Corporation, 1957.

Index

Numbers in **boldface** refer to pages with photographs.

195